DARTS UNLIMITED

DARTS UNLIMITED

Robert McLeod and Jay Cohen

GROSSET & DUNLAP
Publishers • New York
A FILMWAYS COMPANY

Illustrations by David Perry

Library of Congress catalog card number: 76-45542
ISBN: 0-448-12887-X (Hardcover Edition)
ISBN: 0-448-12886-1 (Paperback Edition)

First printing
Printed in the United States of America

We extend special thanks to the top American players who helped us write this book and provided the entire darting community with their tips and insights for your game's improvement. And, the archives and files of the United States Darting Association, which provided us with a tremendous amount of information and many of the pictures used in the book, were invaluable.

We sincerely hope that *Darts Unlimited* will make the exciting world of darts more fascinating for you.

Bob McLeod/Jay Cohen

CONTENTS

FOREWORD

What sport was played both on the *Mayflower* in 1620 and on the Skylab as it orbited the earth in 1972? If your answer is darts, you're right. Darts is on its way to becoming a major sport in the United States. In Great Britain it is second only to fishing as the most popular pastime.

To many of us, darts recalls the dart set we got as a present when we were youngsters; we thus tend to associate darts with children's games. This is far from the truth, however, as evidenced by sky-rocketing purses at the major darts tournaments being held all over America.

Many different games can be played with darts. All are based on the idea of throwing a small missile, usually with a shaft pointed at one end and feathers on the other, at a target, or dartboard. The type of darts used, the nature of the dartboard, and the distance the thrower stands from the board may vary, but the object of the game is always the same—accuracy. A successful dart player must be able to place a missile that can be no longer than 8 ¼ inches into a specific spot that may measure only a few millimeters. To do this well requires a great deal of hand-eye coordination as well as intense concentration.

The 1975 U.S. Open champion, Conrad Daniels, says, "An important part of the game's great appeal is that anyone can play and play well. Speed and strength are not determining factors. Anyone can become a good competitive player within three months of taking up the game seriously."

Since concentration and coordination are the two most vital assets of the good player, men and women are able to compete on equal terms. Strength or size has no bearing in darts play. Can you imagine a woman tennis player, golfer, or swimmer seriously challenging male players for a single United States Open title? In darts this is not only a possibility, it is a reality.

Darts has become popular for many reasons. The expense involved in purchasing equipment is very low; you can set up a dart court in your home or apartment for less than $50. And you don't need much space for it. In fact, dart courts have been installed in doctors' waiting rooms, photography studios, offices, and, of course, umpteen thousands of pubs.

You can teach yourself the sport in a matter of hours. The degree of proficiency you attain is controlled only by your desire and willingness to pay the price for excellence—practice. And to play or practice you don't need a partner or have to leave your home. Dart players enjoy another added benefit: The intense concentration needed to hit the desired mark on the board enables them to forget daily cares and problems and relax completely. What more can anyone ask of their leisure-time activity? Low cost, ease of learning, and relaxation—darts may be the perfect sport for you!

Darts is also an excellent family game. With practice, children can compete on equal terms with their older siblings as well as with their parents. In no other sport does the whole family have the opportunity of participating on an equal footing.

All in all, once you've tried this fascinating sport you will agree it has a very special magnetism. Whether you decide to become world champion or simply play for the fun of it, darting will become an important part of your life.

DARTS UNLIMITED

DARTING THROUGH HISTORY 1

Long before even the earliest civilizations arose, man learned that by sharpening the end of a strong stick he could produce an efficient tool. With this tool he could kill the wild animals that threatened him and also supply himself with meat. With it he had a weapon that he could use when he was attacked by other men. One can easily imagine some remote ancestor throwing his newly invented spear at a target on the cave wall to perfect his skills. After all, when you are menaced by a wild animal or an enraged enemy, it is important that your first throw hits its mark.

History recounts how human beings improved their spears, first by placing a sharpened piece of flint at the end of the stick and later by replacing the wooden stick with metal. But how far and how accurately could one hurl such an object? We don't know when man learned to place feathers on the end of his spear, but in Aesop's fable of the Eagle and the Arrow, which dates back to the sixth century B.C., the eagle laments that his mortal wound was caused by a dart, the shaft of which contained eagle feathers.

As weapons of war, spears and arrows were common in the ancient world. The bow and arrow has been a potent weapon for thousands of years. One story relates the woes of a Saxon king who was so short that he couldn't use the bow and arrow. A king who could not fight for his throne would not hold it for long, so the king and his counselors had to find a way for the monarch to show his prowess. They sawed off the ends of arrows and left the king with missiles about a foot long. As he led his men into battle, the king hurled these projectiles at the enemy. Thus the dart was born.

The use of darts in sport can be traced back to the fifteenth century when the light flight arrows of the English bowmen were adapted for an indoor version of a game called "the butts." For this sport, the rounded ends, or butts, of wine casks were used as targets for the shortened arrows, or "dartes." The new sport gained adherents among commoners and nobles alike. Even Henry VIII found time during his turbulent reign to show an interest in the game. We know that Anne Boleyn gave her fickle king a set of jewel-encrusted darts for his birthday.

During the seventeenth century there are references, in the *Mayflower's* logs, to darts as a pastime of the Pilgrims on board the vessel. Further evidence of the popularity of darts around this time can be found in the writings of William Shakespeare, who mentions a "dart of chance" in *Othello.* The dartboard as we know it, with its divided clock face, was also in use by this time.

A Saxon king was too short to use the bow and arrow. He had his problems solved by the invention of the dart.

In Britain, each region developed its own style of dartboard in the 1800s. These boards were all based on the clock, or pie, concept, but the "slices" were of different sizes. Even today, a trip around Britain will uncover such boards as the Irish, the Yorkshire, the Manchester, or the London Clock. One major manufacturer of dartboards makes five different boards to keep its customers happy. Nevertheless, all the major British tournaments are played on the standard eighteen-inch, twenty-number clock-face board with double, triple, and bulls-eye scoring areas.

The popularity of darts in Great Britain has never waned. Over 7 million people there are considered to be serious dart players today. This ranks darts as Britain's second most popular sport—only fishing out-ranks it.

Although the difficult life of the American colonists precluded most sports, taverns and roadhouses in the colonies had their dartboards and dart players who were seeking a way to socialize and relax. Only recently, however, has the game caught on in the United States as a sport. Today there are more than 3.7 million serious players in the States. In the early years of play, the Americans developed their own dartboard and their own type of game. American-style darts is still

played in many parts of the United States, particularly in Pennsylvania and in upstate New York areas. This game involves throwing for points only and stresses accuracy through repetition of the throwing motion. But there is little strategy involved, and it is not difficult to understand why many American players are switching to the English version of the game. Instructions for playing several versions of darts can be found in chapter 4.

Charlie Young, a top-ranked player from Philadelphia, is among those responsible for bringing English darts into the American game. Young found something lacking in the American-style game he was playing; it required absolutely no thinking, just a good "stroke." When he was introduced to the English game he became an enthusiastic disciple of the English version and proceeded to convert many of the top American-style players to it. Young tells everyone that the appeal of English darts is that "the mind is always working. One gets totally involved in the sport."

In any event, back to our darting history. In the early 1900s, patents were issued for the first all-metal dart and for many different kinds of flights. It is interesting that a number of these patents were issued to Americans. At this time, darts also officially became a sport where skill rather than chance determined the outcome of a contest. British law was responsible for the new designation. The law prohibited games of chance in public houses (taverns). When a magistrate claimed that darts could therefore not be played at the pubs, the dart players of Britain actually instituted work slowdowns and other forms of protest. At the trial of one dart player, the defendant set up a dartboard in the courtroom and immediately threw three darts into the double-20 area of the board. He challenged the magistrate and prosecuting attorneys to duplicate the feat. They could not. The court thereupon decided that darts was indeed a sport and not a game of chance and could be played in the pubs.

There are unconfirmed reports that darts helped win the First World War. Apparently the newly organized Royal Air Force felt that their most formidable weapon against the lumbering German zeppelin was the dart. Can you imagine a German pilot trying to explain to his superiors how his gas-filled craft was shot down?

By the 1930s darts had established itself as a drawing-room sport for Britain's high society. This social status reached its peak in 1937 when King George VI and Queen Elizabeth competed against each other at the Slough Social Centre. In 1939, the fervor for social darting was such that it almost forced the Chamberlain government into crisis quite apart from its already serious international problems. Magistrates in Scotland saw fit to ban the sport in pubs on the theory that it fostered too much "ne'er do-wellism" among the working men. The public outcry that arose found its way to the floor of Parliament. There, the Home Secretary, Sir Samuel Hoare, made such a strong speech in favor of darts that the sport was restored to the pubs once again.

During World War II many American servicemen stationed in Great Britain became familiar with darting. When they returned home after the war, they brought a knowledge of and liking for the game with them. It should also be noted that during the war, dart clubs throughout Britain held tournaments to raise money for the Red Cross and collected well over a million dollars.

In 1959 a group of Americans stunned the dart world when the crew of the liner *United States* defeated the crew of the British *Queen Elizabeth* in a much publicized match in New York City. Matters returned to normal the following year when the crew of Britain's *Queen Mary* recaptured the unofficial darts championship of the seagoing world by drubbing the *United States'* crew in a rematch.

Until recently, the British have rightfully considered themselves to be the masters of the sport. But during the late 1960s, dart leagues sprang up in a number of American communities. Leagues could be found in Los Angeles, Detroit, Dallas, New York, San Diego, San Francisco, Cleveland, Atlanta, Philadelphia, Boston, and many other cities and small towns. In 1969 the United States Darting Association

A poster announcing the first USDA Open Championships. The prizes included a television set, a suit of clothes, dinner for two, and trophies. The 1976 USDA Open also had trophies—plus prize money totaling $18,500.

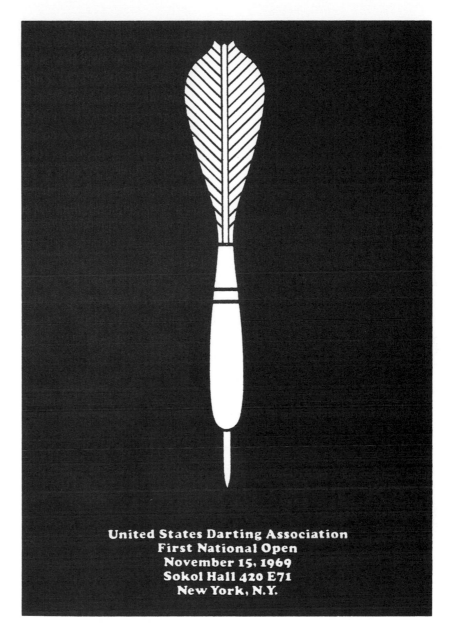

United States Darting Association
First National Open
November 15, 1969
Sokol Hall 420 E71
New York, N.Y.

was founded. This organization, along with the leagues, began to produce and sponsor tournaments where American players gained the opportunity to hone their skills through competition. In the early days the tournament prizes were TV sets, luggage, and the like; today, purses of $30,000 and more are played for. Consequently, the Americans' skills have increased tremendously.

In 1970, former *News of the World* Champion Barry Twomlow defeated the 1969 U.S. champion, Kirk Dormeyer, a New York stockbroker, in a challenge match held in New York City. But when Twomlow, an Englishman, returned to the United States in 1971, he was overwhelmed by the brilliant play of the reigning U.S. champion, Bob Thiede. And two time U.S. Champion, (1973-74), Al Lippman, who was the first American to compete in the *News of the World* Championship, easily defeated the tournament's favorite in 1974, much to the dismay of the English supporters. America's advance in the sport was beginning.

In 1974, a very strong American team defeated a hand-picked British side in a fifteen-match heads-up competition. The score was 9−6. The match, which was held at the British-owned Royal Manhattan Hotel in New York City, left the entire darting world stunned. One member of the British side was heard to admit that the "Americans were getting bloody good at darts." Another shock to the British in 1974 was the fact that American George Silberzahn, from Gibbstown, New Jersey, won the first USDA International Classic even though the British had sixty-one of their best players in the field. This just couldn't be happening! At the end of this tournament the frustrated British tried to gain some consolation by offering to match their best player against one of America's best in one game of 3001. To make the match more interesting, each side put up $1,000. Again it was to be an American victory as Philadelphia's Ray Fischer defeated Britain's number-one player, Welshman Alan Evans.

The program cover from the challenge match between the United States and Great Britain held March 15, 1974.

'Tons' of luck to the teams of Great Britain and the U.S.A.

Jameson Irish Whiskey
Dublin, Ireland

The official results of the 1974 heads-up competition between the United States and Great Britain. The Americans won, 9 matches to 6.

GAME	PLAYER NO.	NAME (UNITED STATES)	PLAYER NO.	NAME (GREAT BRITAIN)	U.S. LEGS WON	GB LEGS WON	U.S. GAMES WON	GB GAMES WON
1	15	N. Virachkul	5	K. Brown	1	2	0	1
2	11	B. Thiede	3	M. Bowell	2	1	1	1
3	12	C. Tinson	17	L. Rees	0	2	1	2
4	14	R. Varian	19	L. Pratchatt	2	0	2	2
5	1	A. Lippman	12	C. Inglis	2	0	3	2
6	13	D. Valletto	14	R. Morgan	2	0	4	2
7	7	J. Macredes	10	P. Gosling	2	0	5	2
8	6	T. Kerr	1	J. Ambler	2	0	6	2
9	2	J. Baltadonis	7	W. Etherington	0	2	6	3
10	9	J. Pacchainelli	16	D. Priestner	2	0	7	3
11	8	J. Ouellette	15	B. Perry	2	0	8	3
12	5	B. Iwanowicz	8	A. Evans	0	2	8	4
13	4	R. Fischer	9	A. Glazier	2	0	9	4
14	3	L. Craig	6	N. Clarke	1	2	9	5
15	10	G. Silberzahn	13	C. Love	1	2	9	6
				Match Result			9	6

On the left, George Silberzahn, winner of the first International Classic. On the right, former U.S. champion Bob Thiede, the first American to have a dart named for him.

Welsh ace Leighton Rees competing at the *News of the World* Championships in London.

But, despite the improvement of American and other players around the world, the British have not yet relinquished the unofficial world championship. Since 1927 this event has been held each spring in London under the sponsorship of an English newspaper, the *News of the World.* The United States and Sweden (where darts is the number-one participant sport) have sent their champions to the match since 1972—without success. Nevertheless, in 1975, U.S. champion Conrad Daniels returned to England two months after losing the world championship and won the annual Champion of Champions Tournament, which is held in Leeds. The Yorkshire television station sponsored the event and invited the sixteen top players in the world to compete. Daniels' win, which was viewed by more than 20 million Britons, is still talked about.

In 1976 a pair of Australians won one of the doubles championships held in England. These losses by the British to the Americans and Australians have been good for the sport of darts. They have attracted world interest in the sport and have served to put the British on notice. And the English have accepted the challenge by playing better darts than ever before.

No history of darts would be complete without mention of its role in the American space program. When our astronauts returned from the moon in 1969, they played darts to help pass the time while they were sequestered in "moondust" isolation. And in January of 1972, darts became a space-age sport when the game went along with the astronauts to help them pass the idle hours during the fifty-two days that Skylab orbited the earth.

WHAT TO BUY
AND WHY

Every form of darts involves throwing a dart at a board, so you need only two basic pieces of equipment: a dartboard and a set of darts. There are three darts in a set. Once you have your darts and your board, you can begin to learn the principles of the sport. As you become more proficient, you may want to add other equipment and accessories, and many items are available—special carrying cases, a dart sharpener, scoreboard, special lighting, and a dartboard cabinet. Virtually all of the high-quality equipment is made in England, although a few American companies are beginning to manufacture some items.

The Dartboard　There are many different kinds of dartboards. Some look like archery or rifle targets; others have pictures of sports fields, such as a baseball diamond or racetrack, imprinted on them. These are *not* the board that the English game is played on. Darts as a sport uses the official English clock board. This board measures 18 inches in diameter and has a 13⅜-inch scoring area that is divided, like a pie, into twenty equal pieces. Each piece is numbered 1 through 20. Darts that hit within the scoring area earn a score equal to the number of the pie piece. This is the single zone. Enclosing the outer circumference of the divided board is a ⅜-inch-wide band between two wires. This is the double zone; if a dart hits within the wires on a pie piece of this zone, it counts two times the value of that particular segment. Roughly halfway between the outer circumference and the center is another band, also ⅜ inch in width, known as the triple zone. A dart that hits between the wires in the zone counts for three times the number of the wedge it is in. At the center of the board are two small circles called the bulls-eye, or cork. The bulls-eye also has two zones; the outer zone is worth 25 points and the inner zone is worth double that amount, or 50 points.

Dartboards can be made of paper, cork, wood, or a sisal bristle. Boards made of wound or compressed paper are similar to some forms of wallboard. These boards are the least expensive and are suitable for the beginner or sometimes player. They can weigh anywhere from ½ pound to about 7 pounds. The material used in their construction does not lead to a long life for this board. Because of the low cost involved in their manufacture, these boards are very often included with the toy dart sets sold in department and novelty stores. Cork dartboards are rather expensive and are usually used as decorative pieces. As playing boards, the cork boards have an even shorter life than paper boards because the cork tends to chip away as the darts strike the playing surface.

The earliest dartboards were made of wood; elm and poplar boards are still widely used in Britain. The elm board must be soaked in water

The official English clock or 20-point dartboard. It is divided, like a pie, into twenty equal pieces.

A dartboard made from compressed paper is often found in toy dart sets. These boards are inexpensive, but they are not thick enough for constant play and have a relatively short life.

The center of the board is divided into two zones, the double bulls-eye and the single bulls-eye. The triple ring is found halfway between the center and the outer circumference of the scoring area. The double zone is the ring that encircles the outer circumference.

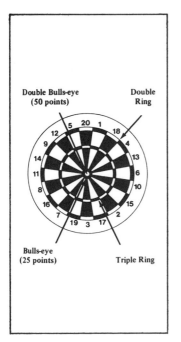

Double Bulls-eye (50 points)

Double Ring

Bulls-eye (25 points)

Triple Ring

every day to prevent it from drying out and splitting, a soaking that can cause the wires to rust. A well-maintained wooden board, however, is excellent to play on because very few darts fall out of, or bounce off, this type of board. It is difficult to match the satisfaction one gets from hearing the solid "Thunk" as your darts hit an elm board. But wooden boards are not recommended for home use because of the difficulty in maintaining them and the mess that the constantly dripping board creates. They are also very heavy, weighing about 18 pounds when wet. The *News of the World* Championship is the only major tournament that still uses this type of board, but it remains a favorite in many English pubs.

Today, most championship play takes place on the bristle board. These boards consist of millions of strands of sisal (hemplike fiber) that have been gathered and compressed. Although many dartists will swear that these boards are made from pig bristle, this has not been the case since 1934 when the sisal bristle board was invented to replace the odorous boards that were made from pig bristle.

The fibers of a bristle board stand on end and resemble the bristles of a brush. This permits the darts to go between the strands rather than stick into them. If you can picture a 1 ½-inch slice of thick rope in cross section, you will have an idea of the mechanics of the boards. The fibers are gathered together, placed in a template, and compressed by hydraulic pressure. The compressed fibers are bonded to a sturdy backing and tied into a unit with a strong steel band. High-tensile steel wire is used for the dividers between the numbers as well

A side view of a bristle board shows its thickness. It is much sturdier than a paper board and can be expected to give many years of use.

as for the bulls-eye and the double and triple zones. These wire dividers, which are called the board's *spider,* will retain their shape for years, even under constant play. This ability to maintain the integrity of scoring divisions is an important advantage of bristle boards over paper or cork boards whose wires bend or become loose with prolonged play. A bristle board weighs 12 pounds and is built to give the average player many years of use.

If you intend to become a serious player, you should purchase a bristle board. In the long run, its initial expense will pay for itself many times over, and it is much more satisfying to play on than the toy models. Maintaining a bristle board is almost carefree, but you must remember to rotate it periodically. This is done by removing the number ring and turning the board two to four wedges to the left or right (keep in mind that segment 20 must always be black), rotating the board around its center-screw axis. Rotating the board ensures that the pie sections of the board that are most often thrown at are not overused. Incidently, a bristle dartboard should never be soaked or treated in any way.

The Dart   Almost all dart games involve throwing three darts for each turn, so a set of darts contains three darts. There are literally hundreds of different kinds and styles of darts. Before you purchase a set, you should try throwing several types of darts to determine which is most comfortable for you. Just as there are tennis rackets and golf clubs to fit almost every individual, there are different darts for different styles of players. Darts differ in weight, balance, length, grip, type of flights (replaceable rear stabilizer), and the material from which the barrel or the flight is

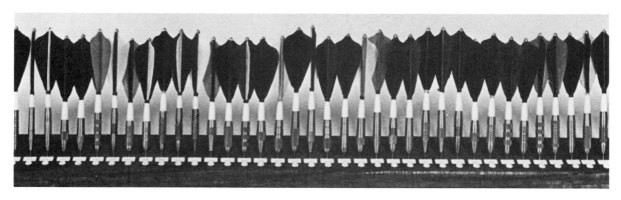

There are many different darts for each person's style.

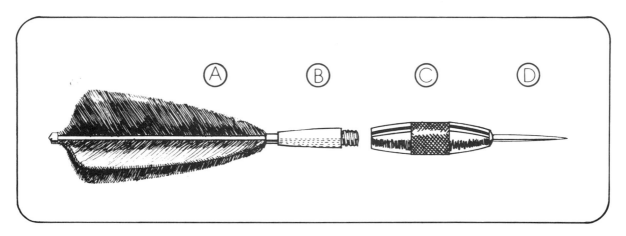

The dart has three basic parts. *A* represents the feathers and *B* the adapter. Together they comprise the flight. *C* is the barrel of the dart, and *D* is the point.

The American board made from hard wood. On this board the double and triple zones are near the outer circumference.

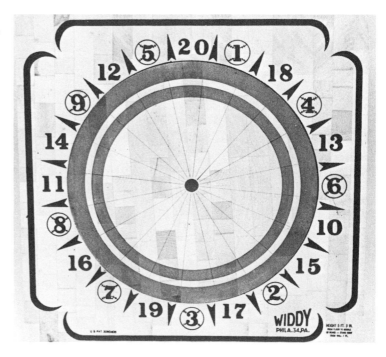

made. Finding exactly the right dart for you could take years of experimenting with various styles and weights, but it is worth searching for.

The dart has three basic parts: the point, the barrel, and the flight. The point of the dart is always made of hardened steel. Darts with long points are preferable to short-pointed darts for two reasons. First, darts with short points can cause dents in the face of the bristle board. These dents are bent fibers, and it doesn't take too many of them to shorten the life of the board. Second, short-pointed darts are apt to bounce off a wire when they strike the board next to a wire. The short point enables the barrel to hit the wire hard, and as a result the dart is sprung from the board. When a long-pointed dart hits a wire, its length enables it to slide past the wire without the end of the barrel touching it, and the dart remains in a scoring area.

Dart barrels are made of wood, plastic, or metal. Wooden darts are required equipment for the American game, which is played on the dry wooden American board. All players in an American game use the same set of darts; each succeeding player retrieves the darts and calls the previous thrower's score. Wooden darts are generally weighted with lead. The biggest problem with this type of dart is the lack of uniformity from dart to dart. The nature of wood makes it difficult to manufacture this type of dart with any degree of uniformity. Wooden darts are inexpensive; they cost about $5 a dozen.

Darts with plastic barrels are also inexpensive, about $1 for a set of three. These darts are easily molded and therefore can be mass produced. Generally they are not consistent in manufacture and are used only as toys.

All serious players of English darts should choose darts with metal barrels. These darts can be turned out on precision lathes, and each dart of a particular model will be uniform in size and weight. Most

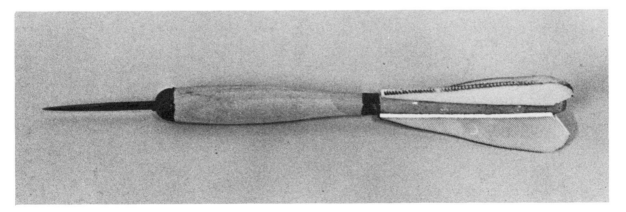

Wooden darts are inexpensive, but they generally lack uniformity from dart to dart.

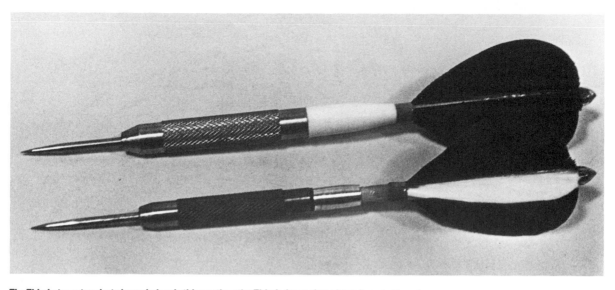

The Thiede tungsten dart shown below is thinner than the Thiede brass dart above it, even though both darts have the same weight.

metal barrels are made of brass, although the use of tungsten alloys and nickel silver for the barrel has recently become popular. Most metal darts weigh from 11 to 45 grams (USDA tournament regulations do not specify a minimum weight and allow a maximum weight of 55 grams). Tungsten makes a good dart barrel because the metal is about twice as heavy as brass, which means a thinner dart—for higher scoring potential—that retains acceptable weight characteristics. A thin brass barrel would weigh less—thus gaining in scoring potential—but lose a good bit of its control in flight. It must be mentioned that thin darts often cause problems with grip that can adversely affect a player's game.

As in all sports, the primary objective in playing darts well is consistency. Generally, a brass dart in the medium-weight range, about 20−26 grams, will serve the average player, the person who plays only for enjoyment for a few hours a week, much better than the thinner darts, which require hours of practice each day to keep one's game in top form. Another drawback to the tungsten dart is its expense. These darts can cost as much as $50 a set, whereas brass darts cost about $5 a set.

Tungsten darts are not necessarily better for good players either. They are thinner for a given weight and therefore it is easier to place all three darts in the small scoring areas of the board. But they are harder to hold and to control. As many players have had their game diminish as those that saw an improvement after switching to tungsten. You must determine whether the increased scoring potential afforded by tungsten darts outweighs any possible loss in consistency.

By the way, there is no such thing as a pure tungsten dart. The tungsten is alloyed with iron and nickel or copper, since pure tungsten is far too hard to be machined on a practical basis. And although extremely strong, tungsten is very brittle; a pure tungsten dart that fell off the board could easily crack or break.

The weight distribution in the barrel of a metal dart gives each style its unique balance. There are three basic balance points for a dart: a dart can be heavy in front, heavy in the middle, or can have its weight evenly distributed. The weight and balance of the dart you select will depend largely on how you throw the dart—hard or soft throw, arc, or flat trajectory—and, most important, how the dart feels in your hand. The law of gravity dictates that a front-heavy dart be thrown harder than a dart that is evenly balanced in weight. The dart with its weight in the front gives the thrower more of a feeling of throwing an object at a target point; evenly weighted darts tend to "float" when you throw them; darts with the weight concentrated in the center give a good push-off point for the fingers to work with the throw. There is no right or wrong balance point; it's a matter of personal preference.

The barrel of a dart comes in several different grips. Some metal darts and all wooden darts are smooth. Metal darts also can be purchased with notches, grooves, or knurling (multithreaded diamond-shaped ridges). Again, the grip you choose depends largely on your own likes and dislikes. But the smoothness of your skin and the amount that you perspire are factors to consider when selecting the proper grip. If your hands perspire freely, you should not choose darts with metal barrels that have been made resistant to corrosion; these include chrome plated, stainless steel, or galvanized iron barrels. What you want is a

A dart can be front heavy (A), heavy in the middle (B), or have its weight evenly distributed C).

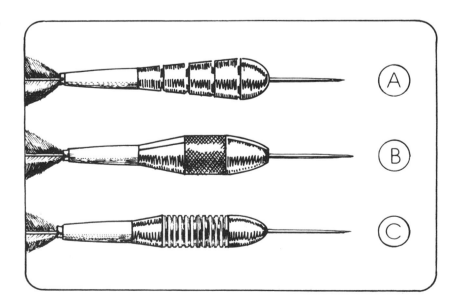

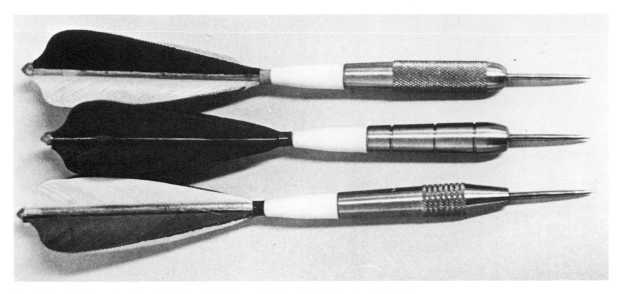

The grip on a dart barrel can be quite different. A dart must feel comfortable in your hand. The dart on the top is knurled, the middle dart is smooth with grooves, and the dart on the bottom has raised ridges.

The same barrel and point can look and perform quite differently with different flights.

metal dart that will react with the salty perspiration that your fingers produce. In time this will erode the dart in such a manner as to produce your own personalized grip. This should be a consideration when purchasing tungsten-based darts as well. A tungsten/nickel alloy gives the dart a better appearance, but these darts can become slippery after prolonged use. Tungsten darts alloyed with copper are softer and will corrode more readily than those alloyed with nickel. The copper alloy becomes slightly abrasive with use, and this produces an excellent grip. One of the top players in the country uses copper/tungsten darts and has slight pitlike sections in his darts where he has placed his fingers time after time.

The flights at the end of each dart vary greatly in material and shape. Many players prefer to use a style and shape of flight that give their darts the smoothest flight to the board. Others concern themselves with the convenience of carrying flights in the pocket, or with visibility when the dart is in the board. Flight lengths differ also. In choosing the style, type, and length of your flights, be guided by what works best for you. You can determine this only through experimenting.

Flights are made from feathers, polyester, plastic, or paper. Paper flights are cheap—you can make your own if you wish—but they wear out rapidly. Polyester or mylar flights are popular. These are used in conjunction with nylon, wood, or aluminum shafts. Some players prefer these flights because they can be easily disassembled and safely placed in a pocket wallet. Plastic flights are made by injection molding into a one-piece unit. They are long-lasting and inexpensive, but they tend to bounce off one another on impact—a problem with polyester or mylar, too—and are reputed not to fly as well as other types of flights. Feather flights, which are made from turkey feathers, are preferred by the top players. At the 1975 USDA Masters Championship, 23 of the top 32 players used feather flights.

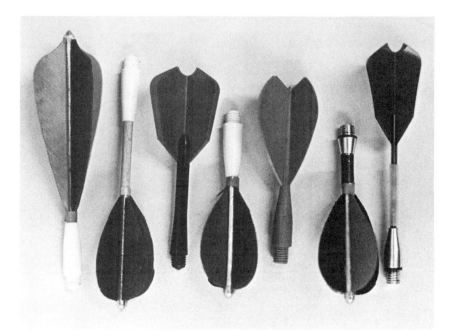

Flights can be made from feathers, plastic, polyester, or paper.

The polyester flights and the rest of the dart can be stored in a convenient pocket wallet.

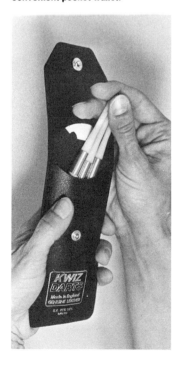

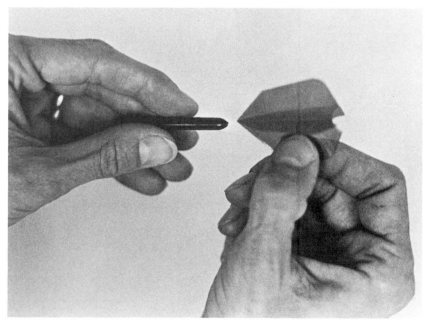

Polyester flights are easily assembled. This makes storage in your pocket a snap.

English craftswomen take painstaking care in producing a set of feather flights. Once made, the flights are inspected, matched, and boxed.

One leading English dart manufacturer imports flight feathers from the stockyards of Chicago. The feathers are cleaned and sanitized, then dyed and cut to shape. This work is all done by hand by craftspersons who must have several months of training before they tackle the job. The cut and dyed feathers are then applied to the flight shaft, which has been coated with a tacky, quick-drying glue. In fact, the glue dries so rapidly that an inexperienced person on the assembly line can create a minor crisis trying to pick up more than one color flight. A little-known fact is that there are left-hand and right-hand feathers, and all the wings on any one flight must be made entirely of either the right or the left type. Should a mixup occur in the right/left feathers on a flight, it will produce an erratic flight in the thrown dart.

When the end of the barrel of a dart strikes the flight of a feather-flighted dart already in the board, it will almost always slip right through and go into the board for a score. Plastic, on the other hand, is solid, and barrel ends that strike plastic flights will be deflected. This can have a big bearing on scores when there is a tight grouping of the three darts. Feather flights also glide better because the air spaces between feathers supply an aerodynamic lift to the flight.

When a dart hits a feather flight it will usually slip right by. A dart that strikes a plastic flight will bounce off it or stick in the flight.

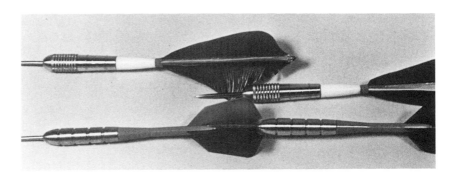

A recent innovation is the Springbak flight. The spring on the shaft of the flight permits the dart to bend away when another dart strikes it.

It's probably impossible to improve on nature's design for flight, but one English manufacturer has added a spring to the feathered flights. These flights are called "Springbaks," and their particular asset is that they permit a tight grouping of darts with little or no deflection since the flights actually spring out of the way for incoming darts.

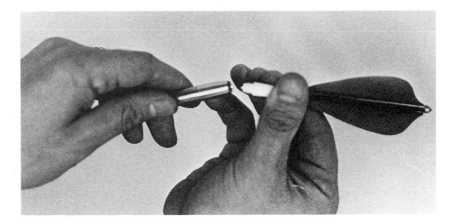

The shafts and adapters that connect the flights to the barrel differ in diameter, length, and composition. Shafts can be made from nylon, wood, fiberglass, aluminum, plastic, piano wire, or some combination of these materials. The adapters that are screwed into the dart barrel come in two different thread sizes: the regular, or ¼-inch, size; the small fitting, or ³⁄₁₆-inch, size. You must get the correct thread size or your adapter will not fit your darts. In general, very light-barreled brass darts and most tungsten darts use the small fitting while the medium-weight and heavier barrels use the regular fitting.

Choosing a Dart Set

As mentioned, you will probably throw a number of different darts before you settle on a model that suits you. Don't worry too much about your initial selection; just make sure that it feels comfortable in your fingers. A few throws of a dart will not really determine what is best for your game. Try your friends' darts whenever you have the chance so that you can catalog in your mind the feel of many different darts. Through trial and experimentation you will eventually find a good dart set for your particular game.

Keep in mind that when you throw at the board, your dart should enter horizontally. If you observe that your darts point downward as they enter the board, try a heavier dart or one with a longer barrel. If your darts point upward when they enter the board, try a lighter dart or one with a shorter barrel. The dart should fly directly to the target and not have a sensation of "floating." If your darts seem to float, you should try a different flight configuration. If your darts wobble or no longer seem to fly true, your flights are probably worn out or damaged in some way and should be replaced. Also, make sure that your dart doesn't slip in your hand as you release it. This will cause the dart to move from side to side or wobble. If this happens, it could be caused by too smooth a grip on your dart, or possibly a grip with too much knurling. Remember, some people's hands are smooth and some rough, some people's hands perspire and some don't. Choose the right grip for your needs.

Weight is always a question when choosing a dart. Generally, players are advised to use light darts when what they are really seeking is a thinner dart. Look at it this way: If you were to throw a marble at the board, you wouldn't have any trouble hitting the target; if you were to throw a feather (i.e., a much lighter object), you would really have to heave it to get it anywhere near the target. The same principle applies with the light dart. The extra thrust necessary to get a light dart to the board usually has a negative effect on the average player's ability to be consistent.

Above all, remember that your darts should fit *you.* Don't be overly influenced by what someone else tells you to buy. You are the one who must hit the mark with the darts you play with. You have no one to blame but yourself if your game isn't as good as you would like it to be.

Other Equipment

Dart Cabinet

For the interior decorators among you, there are dart cabinets to house your dartboard. These cabinets, usually equipped with a scoring area inside the doors, will serve to decorate even the most fashionable of homes. But they are particularly valuable to the owner of a small home, or the apartment dweller who has no space to hang a dartboard except the living room. Dart cabinets are usually easy to hang, requiring only a couple of nails or screws.

A dart cabinet enables you to decorate the area around your dartboard. On the inside of the door there is a chalkboard for scoring.

Lighting   In order to get the full enjoyment out of playing, and to play as well as you are capable of playing, your board should be lit properly. Proper lighting is a must when you are setting up a dart court. The best method of lighting is to put the source of light directly over the dartboard so that the light beams down onto the board. The light should be on the board only, with no diffusion to the sides or back toward your eyes. You want a good clear view of the dartboard. The light should be about 150 watts but intensely focused on the playing area. The two best lighting systems utilize a high-intensity lamp or two fluorescent rods of light. Spotlights are not good; they tend to dry out the board, usually give too much light, and the heat they generate develops convection air currents that affect the flight of a dart.

Backboard   A good backboard, sometimes referred to as a *surround,* is about 32 inches square and can be made from almost any stiff board. Backboards can be purchased ready-made, but it is easy to make your own. Try a piece of plywood, ¼ -to ⅛ -inch thick, cut to size. Mount your dartboard hanging bracket in the middle of the board, adjust the bracket to the regulation height (5 feet 8 inches), and secure the backboard in place. Stain or otherwise cover the plywood so that the backboard will fit the room's decor.

You will need a backboard to protect the wall on which you hang your dartboard.

A dart mat will protect your floors and also give you the correct throwing distance.

Dart Mat A dart mat is similar to a carpet runner. It is made of rubber or polyvinyl. The toe line imprinted on the mat gives the players the correct throwing distance. These mats are excellent for protecting your hardwood floors from errant darts and also for protecting the darts from a concrete floor if your darting area is in the basement. A dart mat also helps round out the complete "dart court feeling" that is nice to experience when you play.

Scoreboard You need some sort of scorecard to keep track of your games. Of course, a piece of paper can be used to keep score, but most players prefer a scoreboard mounted close to the dartboard and easily seen by all the players. Many pubs use chalkboards for scoring, but you may not want the chalk dust in your home. One good alternative is a lucite scoreboard on which the markings are made with an easily erasable grease-type marker.

Dart Sharpener All that practice and all those games you are playing will eventually dull the points of your darts. Improper sharpening can ruin dart points. Dartists use a special pocket sharpener developed just for keeping dart points in top shape. Always carry a sharpener with you to remove any burrs that may develop or to repoint a dull dart, but keep in mind

This lucite scoreboard can be written on with an erasable crayon-type marker.

Turn Score		_01	Team	CRICKET	Team		Turn Score		_01
				Bulls-Eye					
				20					
				19					
				18					
				17					
				16					
				15					

For maximum efficiency, a dart should be properly sharpened with a dart sharpener.

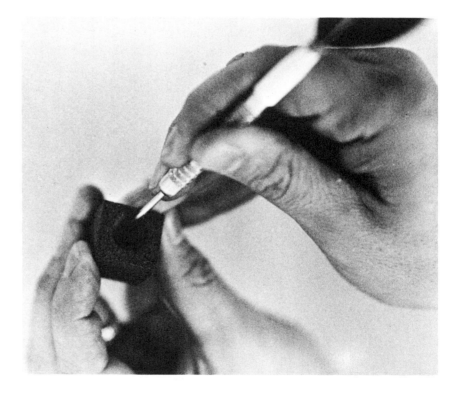

that darts can be too sharp. New darts are always too sharp; practice with them a bit until the point wears down somewhat. Dart points should be somewhat sharper than the point of a slightly used pencil and not as sharp as a needle. When your dart is too sharp it is more likely to bounce off a wire, resulting in no score for that dart. A slightly worn point allows the dart to slide to either side of a wire as it makes impact. Any dart that hits the apex of a wire will bounce off. Only those darts that hit slightly to either side of the top of the wire will be influenced by the sharpness of the points. If your darts are too blunt, they may not penetrate the board's fibers, especially on a slightly worn board. A dart sharpener is a necessary accessory for keeping your darts in good order.

Dart Carrying Case   Darts are sharp and feathers are fragile, so you won't want to carry them loose in your pocket. A good set of brass darts comes with a plastic carrying case. Some players have custom-made leather cases, which they sometimes adapt to attach to their belt like a holster, or a wooden carrier. The newest dart carrier is a leather wallet that can be used with the nylon shaft/polyester flight combination and disassembled for compact carrying in a purse or a suit jacket.

Dart carrying cases are made of wood, molded plastic, or leather.

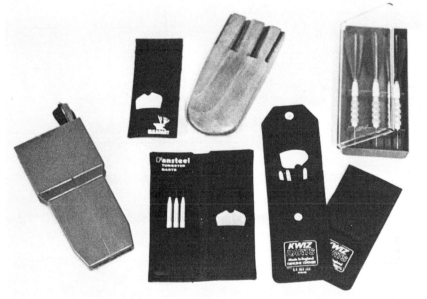

Patches and Posters   Many tournaments offer distinctive cloth-embroidered patches to commemorate the event. These patches can be worn by players on their shirts when they play. Local leagues and other organizations also offer colorful patches with their logos on them. In general you can obtain a tournament patch only by competing in the particular event, but league patches can usually be purchased directly from the leagues. Sometimes the colorful and ingenious posters used to announce tournaments are also available for sale. Both posters and patches have become collector's items for players. They are colorful and decorate a dart court well.

Clothing   Many dart teams wear distinctive uniforms, but no special clothing is needed to play darts. The player should be comfortable, and clothing should be selected with comfort in mind. Shoes should have little or no heels, since heels tend to put stress on the foot and on other parts

Most dart tournaments offer distinctive patches.

of the body. A shirt or vest with proper dart-holding pockets is sensible darting wear. Many of these shirts and vests have colorful designs and pictures on them. For tournament play, the USDA has instituted a formal dress code: men must wear full-length trousers, shoes, and collared shirts; women may wear dresses or blouses and skirts or slacks.

Dart shirts and vests with names and pictures have become very popular.

WHAT TO BUY AND WHY

Dart Toys Children should never be allowed to play with darts unless an adult is there to supervise play. Darts, like knives, forks, and garden tools, can be dangerous around little children. Just as children are taught to use other everyday items safely, they should be taught to use darts safely. One big mistake many parents make is to allow their small children—those less than 3 feet tall—to throw weighted darts at a regulation-height dartboard. These children have to stand very close to the board in order to reach it. A dart that falls from the board will fall point down, which could result in serious injury to a child looking up to admire his feat of throwing. Little people should play on little dart courts; the board should be lowered to eye level and the toe line brought in accordingly. Properly supervised, darts make a terrific pastime for children.

A number of games on the market are similar to darts but do not use steel-pointed darts. These are meant primarily for children who play unsupervised or for groups of adults as a party game. One type of toy dart game has a feltlike board onto which darts with adhesive hooks can be made to stick. Another utilizes magnetic darts, which are thrown at a metal target. These games are fine for children but are not taken seriously by the avid dartist.

SETTING UP A DART COURT

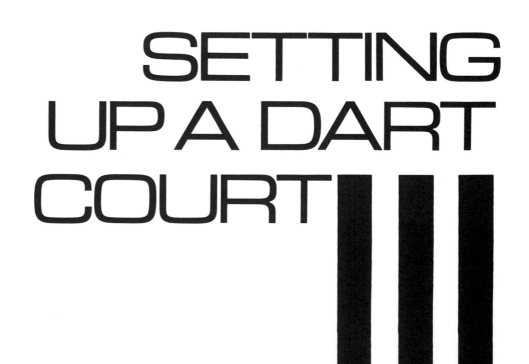

Any athletics field has its required dimensions, and a dart court is no exception. Sport fans know that a football gridiron or a baseball diamond has a certain look that is unique for the particular activity. This is also true for a dart court. It is unlikely that you will build a special dart room or devote a room exclusively to playing darts, so the manner in which you set up your darting area must depend largely on where you put it and how decorative or authentic you want it to be. This chapter gives you the "musts" and a few suggestions to help the dart court fit better in your home. Fortunately, darting equipment is in itself interesting looking, and with a little ingenuity on your part it can be deployed in such a manner as to make your darting area a conversation piece in your home. Once the basic measurements are established, the rest is up to your own imagination.

Where to Place Your Court

Where you place your dartboard will be determined by the space available to you and your decorator's sense. There is no one right place. In New York City apartments, space is often at a premium, and dartists hang their boards wherever they can find the minimum footage. The rules of New York's Knickerbocker Dart League simply state that a dart court must be 3 feet wide with 8 feet from the face of the board to the toe line; the dartboard must be 5 feet 8 inches from the floor to the center of the bulls-eye and lighted adequately. This permits league play on courts with a minimum amount of space to devote to darting. On the other hand, the life style of people in Southern California is based on plenty of room for everyone. Therefore players in this area usually have more space allotted for their playing area. The rules of the Southern California Darts Association insist that the darting area be at least 10 feet long with 2 feet of clear space on either side of the 3-foot-wide toe line. In effect this means a minimum playing area of 10 feet x 7 feet.

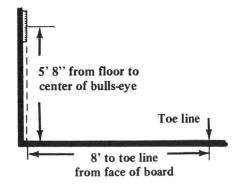

5' 8" from floor to center of bulls-eye

Toe line

8' to toe line from face of board

The dartboard is mounted so that there is a distance of 5 feet 8 inches from the floor to the center of the bulls-eye. The toe line is 8 feet from the face of the board.

Let's see where you might place your board. A family room is ideal. The family room is the center of activities, and you will want to make darts a family activity. Allot an area that is roughly 5 feet x 10 feet with the 10-foot length perpendicular to the wall on which your board will be mounted. Remember, *never* place your board on the back of a door unless it is a closet door. If someone opened the door just as a throw was being made, a serious injury could occur.

You might want to construct your dart court in the basement of your home. Setting up the dart court might be just the excuse you need to start finishing off the basement—a job that never seems to get under way.

Hanging a dartboard is a much greater problem in an apartment, where most of the living space is already taken. Here a closet door often comes in handy. Or if you have space in your living room, you might consider hanging the board enclosed in a decorative cabinet. Some dart cabinets are so attractive that, when closed, they are admired as wall hangings. One dartist commissioned an oil painting on the outer doors of his dart cabinet, so it would blend in with the rest of the apartment's decorations.

If you set up your darting court in your living room, you should seriously consider purchasing a dart mat. It can be easily rolled up and stored when not in use, and it protects your carpeting from the heavy concentration of foot traffic to and from the board or keep your polished floors from being damaged by poorly thrown darts.

If you play darts in your living room, you might consider hanging your board in a decorative cabinet such as the ones shown.

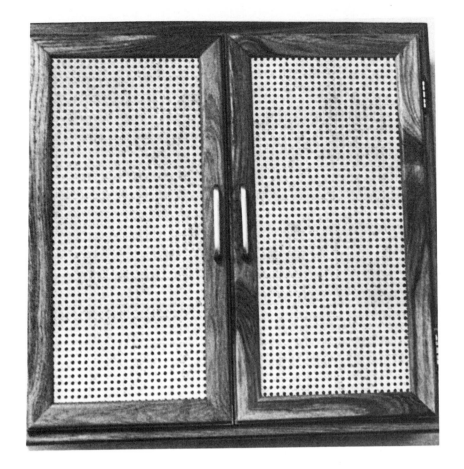

Some darters have converted their garages into playing areas. A garage is an ideal place to play darts. And playing outdoors can be fun also, especially for a group of people. The wind and the vast expanse for a side vision reference point offer new challenges to the dartist, as well as a few laughs.

Pubs or athletic clubs that want to put up dartboards should be especially sure to hang them away from the flow of traffic. In some clubs, and in all of tournament halls, portable dartboard stands are used. Some of these units are completely self-contained with board-hanging bracket and toe line attached by a hinge device so that they can be set up in a matter of minutes. Others are just free-standing backboards for which a toe line must be measured or a dart mat used. In either case, the units can be disassembled and stored.

Remember, it doesn't matter where you set up your dart court, or how, as long as the critical playing measurements of board height and throwing distance are maintained.

The Dimensions   Your standard 18-inch English clock board must be mounted 5 feet 8 inches from the floor to the center of the bulls-eye. The throwing line, toe line, or hockey must be 3 feet wide and 8 feet, measured parallel to the floor, from the face of the board to the foot edge of the line. In

Portable dartboard stands make it possible to remove the dart court when the space is needed for something else.

England, the distance from board to toe line varies from 7½ feet to 9 feet depending on which county you happen to be playing in, but the 8-foot toe line is the distance the players throw from in the unofficial world's championship. The 8-foot distance is standard clear across the United States and in every country in the world except England.

In addition to the actual playing area there should, if possible, be some open space to the outside of the playing lane and a few extra feet behind the player. This area should be away from any through traffic that the room might get, such as having the playing area adjacent to a hallway or bathroom.

Hanging the Board   Before you affix a board to a wall, you will probably want to pad the wall with some sort of protective device. A backboard or dart cabinet works very well. These can be homemade or purchased commercially. If you plan to make your own, a few tips might be helpful. Dark colors reflect almost no light, consequently, a dark backboard will allow you to focus much more clearly on the target area. We have been in a few pubs where the owners have used a reversed truck tire, which has been cut into two pieces, to surround the dartboard. These tires were painted stark white, absolutely the worst color that could have been chosen. The reflected light from the tire really makes it almost impossible and very hard on the eyes to focus properly on the target. Had the tire been left black, it would have been just fine.

In addition to the critical color scheme for the backing, you want to keep in mind that you need a backboard in which errant darts will embed themselves. If the darts do not stick into the backing area, they will bounce about and could cause a nasty accident around your dart court.

Once the backing is in place, you are ready to install your dartboard. Remember, the board must be 5 feet 8 inches from the center of the bulls-eye to the floor. When you buy your bristle dartboard there will be a mounting bracket and three screws affixed to the front of the board. Remove these from the board. Two of the screws are used for mounting the bracket to the wall, and the third screw fits in the center of the back of the board. If your board has a hook or loop at the top, a nail driven through it and into the wall will hold the board in place. The number 20 is always uppermost and either black or the darker color of your board.

A new dartboard has a bracket attached to its face. Use this to fasten the board to the wall, cabinet, or backboard.

Once your board is in place, you can think about lighting it properly. A good lighting system illuminates the board brightly without casting heavy shadows on the board. The lights you use should not impede the flight of a dart in any way. A good light to use would be one that is small, produces intensive light, yet gives off a minimum amount of heat. Heat can affect the flight of thrown darts. Many dartists prefer the high-intensity lamp used to light the dartboards at USDA tournaments. These are compact, give a bright, concentrated light, are relatively cool, and have an adjustable neck. Other players prefer two rods of fluorescent light. Fluorescent lighting is cool and has the added benefit of casting absolutely no shadows, but you must remember to use two lights because a single light produces a flicker that you will notice as you try to focus on the target area. Whatever system you decide to use, it must be one that directs its light to the dartboard only. Any leakage or side lighting that can be seen by the players when they stand at the toe line will adversely affect their game.

Next comes the scoring device and area. Most players prefer to have the score posted directly in front of them when they are on the line. If this is what you want, put the scoreboard as close to the dartboard as you can. Probably the best type of scoreboard for the home is one made from lucite or plexiglass that has the scoring grid printed right on it. An erasable crayon-type marker can be used. If you don't care about chalk dust, you might place a small blackboard near the dartboard.

The dartboard and scoreboard are up, and the lighting is all set—now it's time to get your toe line in place. Since the dartboard has some thickness, the distance from the wall to the toe line will be some inches less than 8 feet if you measure from the wall. To be absolutely accurate, you should drop a plumb line from the center of the board to the floor. From this point on the floor, measure 8 feet and make a mark that will serve as your toe line. A piece of wood 3 feet wide can set a permanent toe line or be a removable fixture on the floor. To protect the floor, consider buying a dart mat—or making one yourself. Many players use a piece of plywood 8 feet long trimmed down to 3 feet wide (from a standard 8 x 4 sheet), which clearly defines your dart court's playing area.

At this point, keep in mind once again that wherever you place your dart court, you must observe any safety precautions that your good sense will determine. For example, seats should not be placed along the 8-foot playing area; encourage spectators to sit or stand *behind* the person who is throwing. And, above all, no dart court in the heavily trafficked areas of your home.

All set? You've choosen your equipment and have your dart court set up. It's time to review the dart games you know and learn about a few more.

GAMES PEOPLE PLAY IV

Any number of games can be played on the standard English dartboard. Here are a few that you might enjoy playing, but you and your friends ought to feel free to invent new games.

For all games played on the English board, the United States Darting Association *Rules and Standards* should be followed. In addition to these basics, many pubs or clubs have house rules, so it is wise to check with one of the locals when playing at a new location. House rules can cover many things; for example, "three in a bed" or a "Shanghai" may automatically win that particular game. You can develop your own house rules, and have a lot of fun with them.

USDA Rules 1. The dartboard for all play is the standard English clock or 20-point bristle dartboard, which measures 18 inches in diameter. The board must be wired with high-tensile steel wire; embedded bands or plastic spiders are not acceptable.

2. The dartboard is mounted 5 feet 8 inches from the floor to the center of the bulls-eye. The toe line, or throwing line, is exactly 8 feet from the face of the board and is 3 feet long running parallel to the board.

The dart player must stand behind the toe line. Both feet must be within the 3-foot-wide line. Many major championships use wooden "wings" to prevent players from going outside this boundary.

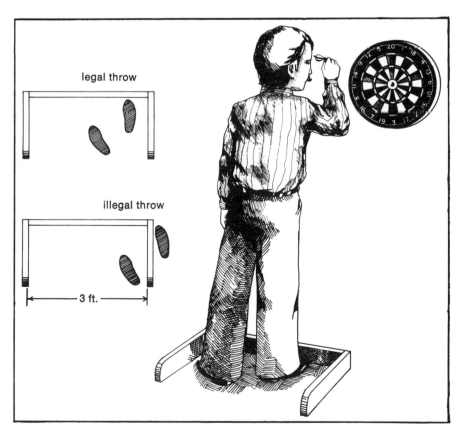

legal throw

illegal throw

3 ft.

3. Three thrown darts constitutes a playing turn. The darts must be thrown by hand, and the player's feet may not cross the throwing line. A player may lean toward the board as far as he likes as long as his feet respect the throwing line. The darts may be as small as the player likes but must not exceed 8¼ inches from the tip of the barrel to the end of the flight nor may they weigh more than 55 grams each, excluding the flight. Nails or other devices may not be used. The dart is understood to have a point, barrel, and a flight-righting fixture (which is generally known as a "flight").

4. To determine the order of play, each player, or one player from each team, throws one dart for the bulls-eye. The dart closest to the bulls-eye wins. A bulls-eye or double bulls-eye is tied by following throws. Those tied must rethrow until the tie is broken. Darts in the single bulls-eye are left in the board; double bulls-eyes are removed to allow room for following darts. The winning player has his choice of order of play. A toss of a coin can also start a game.

5. All thrown darts count. Darts that fall from, are knocked out of, or miss the board, receive no score but do count as thrown darts. Any dart that sticks in another dart also counts as a thrown dart that receives no score. In case a dart lies atop other darts, the idle dart does not score. The point of the dart must enter the face of the board to score.

Any dart that sticks in another dart counts as a thrown dart but receives no score.

All darts are scored at the point of entry. This dart does not score because it is on the wrong side of the 20 wire.

6. All darts are scored at the point of entry. A reading must be taken before the darts are removed from the board. Whichever side of the wire a dart is thrown to is that dart's score. Often a dart will appear to score a value other than it actually gained by entering the board at the color separation between innnings. The wire and not the color distinctions determines a score.

Games

301 The classic English pub game is 301. The aim of the game is to score exactly 301 points by starting on a double and finishing on a double. At the start of the game, 301 points are given to each player. All subsequent scores are subtracted from 301—they are subtracted rather than added up from zero because of the end-game strategy (discussed in detail on pages 96–97). In effect, you must be able to see at all times exactly what you need to arrive at zero.

To start the game, any double will do. To finish the game, the double has to equal the number of points needed to go out exactly (i.e., to reach zero). Each player must get an opening double before he can start accumulating a score.

The double bulls-eye may be used to start or finish a game.

Example: A player starts his score by hitting any double on the board. Darts thrown before the double is hit do not count; *all* darts thrown after the double is hit do count. When a double is hit, the scored amount is subtracted from 301: If the player hits a double 8, he subtracts 16 from 301 and is left with 285. The player continues to throw in turn, subtracting the total score of his three darts from the score at the end of his last turn. He can win the game only by getting a double that gives him a total score equalling the total amount left: With 32 points to go, a double 16 will end the game. A single 16 will still leave 16 to go, which can be gotten by throwing a double 8, and so on down the line. If an odd number is thrown, another odd number is needed to get back to a double possibility. If one less or one more than the exact score is hit, the player must assume the same score he had before his turn was up. (This is called *busting*.)

A perfect 301 game can be scored by using as few as six darts.

501

501 is basically the same game as 301 except that it is played with a straight start (no double is needed to start scoring) and a double finish. This is the official tournament game of the USDA. 501, or any long game, tends to give a winning edge to the better player; there is an element of luck involved in getting a double, and a good player may have to give up a few turns of scoring by not getting that oftentimes elusive starting double needed in 301. In the longer game the better player reduces his score much more quickly than the weaker player, because the better player can consistently throw higher scores. This allows the better player more opportunity at the end of the game to score the winning double.

Other 01 Games

You can play 01 games from any number. For team play, 801 and 1001 are very popular. These games can be played with either a double start or a straight start (sometimes referred to as a *flying start*), but all forms of 01 games end on a double.

Baseball

Any number of individuals or a team may participate in baseball darts. In individual play, each player throws three darts an inning in a regulation 9-inning game. Only the darts that hit the number of the inning being thrown counts as "runs" for that inning. The winner is the player or team with the highest accumulated score for all nine innings.

A player can go out in any 01 game with three darts. If he has 112 points left, he first throws at the triple 20 *(top left)*. Hitting this leaves him with 52 points (112 minus his score of 60). He then hits a single 20 *(top right)*, leaving only 32 points. The final, or game, shot is a double 16 *(bottom left)* which, when hit, will reduce the score to zero.

(Bottom right) This player has "busted." He had 8 points left. His first throw hit a single 4, leaving him with 4 points to make. He next hit a single 2, leaving 2 points. But his third dart hit a single 1. Since you cannot double out on this number, his score reverts back to 8 points.

Example: In the 3rd inning, a player hits a triple 3, a single 3, and a 17. The score for that inning would be 4 runs, one run for the single and three runs for the triple he has hit. The 17 hit does not score.

In team play, all the members of each team throw their three darts each before the next team throws and the innings score is totaled. Tied games require extra innings. In Baseball, it is an advantage to throw last because in the last inning's play you know just what is needed for a win. The pressure of having to score as many runs as possible is taken off you. It is easier to score a game-winning single in the last inning and avoid a possible no-score, which often happens when a player is pressing for triples.

Bulls-Eye Baseball

Playing and scoring this game is the same as for Baseball, except that each player or team takes a turn throwing three darts at the bulls-eye before throwing for the inning. At least one bulls-eye must be scored before any runs can be scored in an inning. And the number of runs scored in an inning is multiplied by the number of bulls-eyes gotten. For teams, one player could be chosen to throw for the inning, or all members of the team could be required to throw for both bulls-eyes and the innings with their individual scores totaled as the score for the inning.

Example: 2 bulls-eyes and 3 runs are scored in an inning; this would be scored as 6 runs. If no bulls-eyes are gotten in an inning, the score for the inning is zero.

Cricket, American

American Cricket is the official doubles game of the USDA and the only game played with darts on the English board where an element of strategy plays an important role in the outcome of the game. All other dart games rely strictly on offense: throwing better darts than your opponent. In Cricket, you can adjust your game to throw for certain numbers that suit you best, or you can jockey your opponent into a position to have to throw for numbers that don't suit his game.

Individuals or teams can play. In team play, a member of one team throws, then a member of the other team throws, and so on. Usually, only numbers 20 through 15 and the bulls-eye are used for the game, although a longer version using numbers 20 through 10 and the bulls-eye is also popular. Each number to be used is called an inning. The object of Cricket is to close all of the game's innings before an opponent does. To close an inning, or number, three of that particular number must be scored. This can be done with one dart in the triple, three singles, or a double and a single of the number. Merely closing, however, does not win the game *if* the opponent is ahead on points. The point deficit, if there is any, must be made up by scoring in live

In Cricket, players throw for the numbers 20 through 15 and the bulls-eye. On the scoreboard each line represents a dart in that number. Team *A* has hit four 20s. Three 20s closed the number, and the fourth 20 counted for 20 points because team *B* has not closed the number.

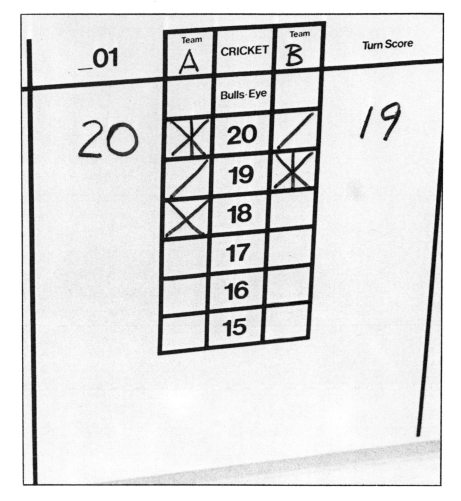

innings. *Important:* Points are not necessary to win; the object is to close the numbers before your opponent does. The player who closes first, even if he has zero points, is the winner as long as his opponent also has zero points. Should the opponent have points, the closed out player must score an equal amount or more points than his opponent before the opponent can close out his numbers. Games cannot end in a tie. A point score for each player that equals 25-25 or any equal number is considered zero score allowing the player who is completely closed out to be the winner.

Example: To close a number, three hits must be scored in that particular number. If one player closes a number before the other player does, every subsequent dart in that number counts for points until the opponent can close the number (e.g. the first player throws his three darts at 20 but only scores two singles with the third dart landing on a non-scoring number. The number is not closed. The second player throws his darts; all three hit in the 20 wedge, a triple and two singles. Thus the second player has closed 20 and has also scored 40 points for the two extra 20s from his total of five hits for his turn. He will continue to receive 20 points for every 20 he subsequently throws until his opponent throws the single 20 he needs to close.).

Remember, to win a game of Cricket you must close all the innings, or numbers, by getting a score of three hits in each number, including the bulls-eye, and you cannot be behind in points.

Cricket is an exciting game for the accomplished player because of the accuracy needed and the strategy involved. Yet it is also an exceptionally good game for the beginner because he is not intimidated by having to get a double before he starts scoring. And darts thrown at one number that land on other numbers being used for the game count for score, or closing. Incidentally, it is this "fall-out" that allows the top-notch player to plan his game strategy. For instance, he might close all the numbers except the 17 and 15 and then throw for bulls-eye, aiming at the lower right portion of the bulls-eye when he throws. By doing this, darts that do not hit the bulls-eye have a chance of falling into 17 or 15 and counting.

Cricket, English

There's a batting side and a bowling side with ten wickets to be taken to make up an inning. Players throw alternately, and each has a turn at both batting and bowling for a complete inning. A predetermined number of innings constitute a game.

On the batting side everything over 40 counts; a 70 with three darts would score 30 runs. On the bowling side each bulls-eye counts as one wicket; a double and single bulls-eye would be three wickets. If a batsman inadvertently throws a bulls-eye, it counts as a wicket for the bowler; if a bowler throws a dart that lands outside the triple zone, the points the dart scores count for the batter.

The batting side continues to score until the bowling side scores their 10 wickets. The roles are then exchanged. The winner is the team with the most points after each team has had an equal number of turns batting and bowling.

51 in 5s

For this game, teams or individuals throw on an alternating basis to obtain a combined total score that is divisible by 5. Each 5 points scored is equal to 1 game point and it takes 51 game points to win. Total scores that cannot be divided evenly by 5 do not count. During the game, darts that miss the board do not count for or against the player. At the final turn, however, the last three darts must all score. It is the last dart that counts in making the total divisible by 5. To go out, all three darts must be used and all must contribute to the score, which must produce the exact number of 5s to total 51.

Example: A player starts with 51 points. In first turn he gets four 20s for 80 points. This score, divided by 5, equals 16. The 16 score is subtracted from the starting 51, leaving 35 game points to go. The game continues until the player has only 3 game points to make. He must then throw all three of his darts and all must score, for a total of 15 points (15 divided by 5 equals 3). A miss or more score than he needs counts as no score, and the player's total reverts back to 3.

14 Stop This game is more interesting when played by two teams although individuals can play assuming both roles of the team function. Any number of teams or persons can play. The first player of the team throws at 14. He must hit 14 or his team does not participate any further in the inning, and no points are scored for that inning. If the first player inadvertently hits 14, he has the option of stopping with that dart or playing his remaining two darts, still throwing for 14. The darts scored in 14 allow the second player of the team to score his darts, which he throws at the number of the inning being played. His score for that inning is multiplied by the number of 14s his partner got. The innings for the game are preselected and can be any number in both quantity and point value. The darts landing in the selected innings count as they do in Baseball.

Example: Player #1 scores three 14s; his teammate then throws for the particular inning that is up and scores 5. The team's score for the inning is thus 3 times 5 (the three 14s multiplied by the inning score) for a total of 15.

The option to stop throwing at 14s can be taken anytime, but it must be exercised before a miss. If three darts are thrown, all three darts must score in the 14. Should player #2 fail to score any hits in the live inning, no matter how many 14s had been scored, the team receives no score for that inning.

Golf Like real golf, the player with the lowest score wins. Sections of the clock dartboard are referred to as *holes*, and each hole is broken down to score as follows: the double zone scores 1; the triple zone scores 2; the area between the triple ring and the bulls-eye scores 3; the area between the triple and double ring scores 4; and darts missing the inning score 5.

The game is either 9 or 18 holes. Players throw at numbers in rotation. But here's the key to the game: *Only the last dart thrown counts for score.* A player may decide to stop his play on each hole whenever he wishes.

Example: Player #1 has scored a 3 by hitting the area between the bulls-eye and the triple ring with his first dart. Right then and there, he declares his first dart to be his last throw. Player #2 follows by throwing his first dart into the same area for 3 points, but he chooses to go for a lower score. He misses scoring with his two remaining darts and has to take a 5 for the hole. He cannot recant and take the score of his higher scoring dart. The maximum score for each hole is 5 (if the last dart thrown is "off the fairway"), and the lowest possible score is a hole-in-one, the double zone.

High Score   Any number of players may play High Score. The object of the game is to get a designated number, usually 1000, before the opponents do. A player does not have to score exactly 1000 to win, but he must score 1000 or more before the opponents accomplish this.

Killer   Killer may be played by any number of players. The object of the game is to "kill" all the other players before you are "killed." The last person remaining in the game is the winner. To start, each player throws for his number with the opposite of his normal throwing hand. This helps to prevent a player from getting his favorite number, or a number that he knows his opponent finds unfavorable. After everyone has a number, play proceeds. Two or more people may have the same number; the number hit on the first throw must be kept for the entire game.

Players throw in turn, decided by any method, and try to eliminate their opponents by hitting the opponents' double ring. Every dart in the double ring counts as 1 point. As soon as a player (or players, if more than one has the same number) has had his number hit five times (for 5 points), he is eliminated. Players may throw at the double ring of any other player. And yes, it is ethical to gang up on the better players to eliminate them quickly. It is also okay for those who are sharing a number to team up to forestall their elimination since all hits in their double ring count against all who share the same number.

If the teamed-up players are the winners, they again throw with their opposite hand to gain a new home number and eliminate the opposition as before. This goes on until there is a single winner for the game. There is one difference in the scores of the playoffs: The number of hits scored in the elimination rounds remains with each player during the final rounds. This way the end game will not drag on with remaining players having to score 5 points each to win.

Mulligan   Mulligan is a difficult game and is usually played by advanced players as a change of pace. Seven random or sequential innings (numbers) and the double bulls-eye are used. Three triples in an inning must be scored before going on the next inning. After the 21 triples are made, three double bulls-eyes are needed to go out. The first player, or team, to get three double bulls-eyes is the winner.

Nine Lives This game may be played by any number of players. Each player has three lives to start the game and is eliminated as soon as he loses them. Innings 1 through 20 are used in order. Each time a player misses an inning with his three darts, he loses one of his three lives.

An alternate game is played the same way except score value of hits is kept with the lowest score for the inning being the one who loses his life. Tied low scores all lose a life. The maximum score for three darts is 9 (3 x 3).

Round the Clock Any number can play. The object is to hit each number, 1-20, and use less darts than your opponents do. The numbers are thrown in numerical rotation. To vary the game, play it by throwing for the double or triple zone instead of just for the number. Or, as it is sometimes played in England, the game may be timed. In 1937, Jim Pike went round-the-clock in doubles, throwing from 9 feet and retrieving his own darts, in 3 minutes and 30 seconds at King John's Head, Blackfriars, London.

Scram Two players or teams can play. One player Stops, the other Scores. The Stopper throws first. He must try and prevent the Scorer from scoring by putting numbers on the board "out of play," which he does by simply landing a dart in a number.

Example: The Stopper throws a 20, 16, and 11 with his turn. These numbers count as zero if the Scorer lands on them.

The Scorer throws, trying to get as much score as possible, avoiding of course those numbers already stopped by his opponent. Play continues until all the numbers on the board have been "stopped." The roles are then reversed, and the player with the higher score wins.

Shanghai Shanghai may be played with any number. Everyone plays individually against all the other players. High score wins the game except when a "Shanghai" is effected. A Shanghai is a triple, double, and single scored in any one inning (number); they may be scored in any order.

The winner of the bulls-eye toss not only has the option of choosing where in the playing order he will throw, but also choosing the numbers that will be used for the game. New numbers are used for every new game. Six random innings, the double and triple rings, and the bulls-eye are used. The scoreboard is aranged in this order: two innings, double, two innings, triple, two innings, bulls-eye. (The winner of the bulls-eye at the start determines what numbers will be thrown for each inning.)

A Shanghai is a single, double, and triple of the same number. Here the player has a Shanghai on 13.

A player must hit the number being thrown for and scores the face value of all his hits; for example, four 17s count 68. If the designated number is not hit, the player's score prior to that inning is halved. When throwing for the double and triple zones, all hits count for score. However, they too must be hit, or the score is halved. This applies for the bulls-eye as well.

Play stops if a Shanghai is scored, and all posted scores are final at that point. The player who scores the Shanghai automatically receives a bonus of 100 points from each player. He totals the points scored on the number of the Shanghai, adds it to his accumulated score, and receives from each player the point difference between his score and their scores. If another player has more points than he has, the Shanghai thrower receives only the 100 bonus points.

NOTE: Any game may be terminated by scoring a Shanghai if this is a "house rule." After two thrown darts, a player may ask his opponent if he may Shanghai. If the rule of Shanghai prevails, the player must declare before his third dart is thrown that he intends to Shanghai. To win on a called Shanghai, the last dart must be thrown for either a double or triple; a single does not win. If the Shanghai is made, the player automatically wins; if it is not, the player does not count any score for that particular inning. This differs from the usual game of Shanghai where the hits may be scored in any order.

Shove Ha'penny   Each player in turn tries to score 3 points in each inning from 1-9. A double counts 2 points and a triple 3 points. All three darts need not be used in any one inning, but a player who scores more than the required 3 points gives his excess points to his opponent, to help the opponent close out his numbers, which are the same. A player cannot win a game by receiving excess points from the opponent. He must score the final point himself.

Sudden Death   Sudden death is an excellent game for eight or more players. It is a game of elimination with the last remaining player the winner. Everyone plays to achieve a high score. Players may throw for any number they choose; however, the lowest score for each turn must drop out. Tied low scores are considered low, and all with that particular score must drop out.

Tic-Tac-Toe   This game is similar to the pencil-and-paper game of the same name. The numbers that form the nine box grid are 12, 20, 18, 11, bulls-eye, 6, 7, 3, and 2.

A player alternates the throwing of one dart with his opponent. The object is to close any three numbers that form a vertical, horizontal, or diagonal line before one's opponent does. If a player needs, for instance, the 3 for a win after closing the 20 and bulls-eye, his opponent can stop him by closing the 3 first. Should ties occur, and they happen as often as with the pencil-and-paper version, the game is a draw and a new game is begun.

You've selected your darts, you know the rules of the games, and your dart court has been set up according to official specifications. You are ready to go. The time has come for you to learn how to make the dart do what you want it to do—get to the exact spot on the board that you want to hit. Throwing from a distance of only eight feet makes the objective sound easy, doesn't it? Well, it's not quite as easy as it sounds.

In America, everyone is brought up on sports. From the time you could walk—perhaps even before—you were taught the correct way to throw a baseball, punt a football, serve in tennis, shoot foul shots in basketball, and kick when swimming. Thus you are aware that there is a right and a wrong way of playing any sport. Darts is no different. You can't simply fling a few darts and expect to be a good player. You must learn certain techniques and basics of form and practice them.

The throwing of a dart can be broken down into several parts, each of which must be mastered separately. When all the parts are combined they should produce a style that will allow you to become a very good player. But remember, in darts as in any sport, your eventual style may vary to a degree from the accepted norm. Your best bet is to learn the basic principles of throwing, then alter them to form your own particular style.

The Grip The generally accepted way to hold the dart is between the first and second finger and thumb. The third finger can be used to steady the point if necessary. The dart should not be pointed at the board like a pencil, the usual mistake that beginners make. The use of the first two fingers, perhaps with the third barely touching the point, gives a firm grip, full control, and keeps the dart from wobbling as it leaves the hand.

Keep in mind that there is no one right way to hold the dart, but it must feel comfortable in your hand so you are able to release the dart easily and without any hitches. Simply grip the dart comfortably. Now, whatever grip you use, you must try to duplicate it exactly every time you throw. Former U.S. champion Conrad Daniels has his darts knurled exactly where he places his fingers. When he was learning to play, he put strips of adhesive tape around his darts so he would be able to place his fingers exactly in the same spots for each throw. Everything about the rest of your throw is affected by your grip on the dart. The weight displacement, trajectory, and the speed of the dart are all controlled by your grip. Accomplished players move their grip forward or aft on the barrel if they want their darts to sail or drop a bit in order to obtain a good score.

Many different grips are used when people throw a dart. Most of the experts utilize the first two fingers and the thumb.

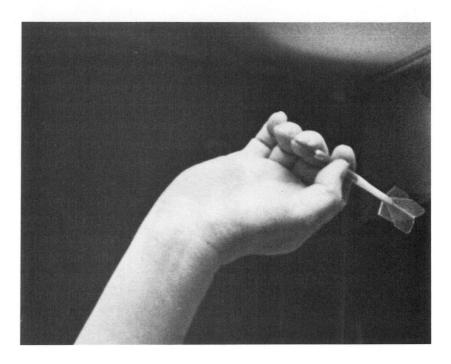

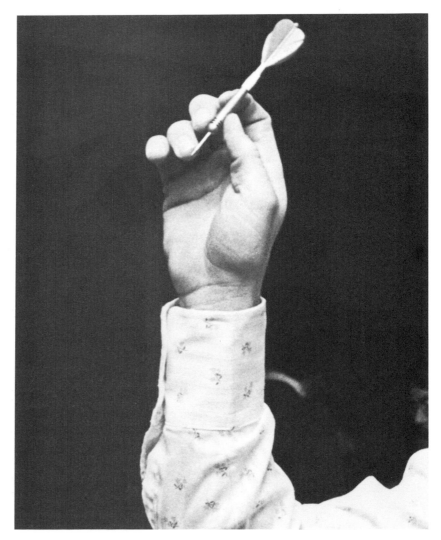

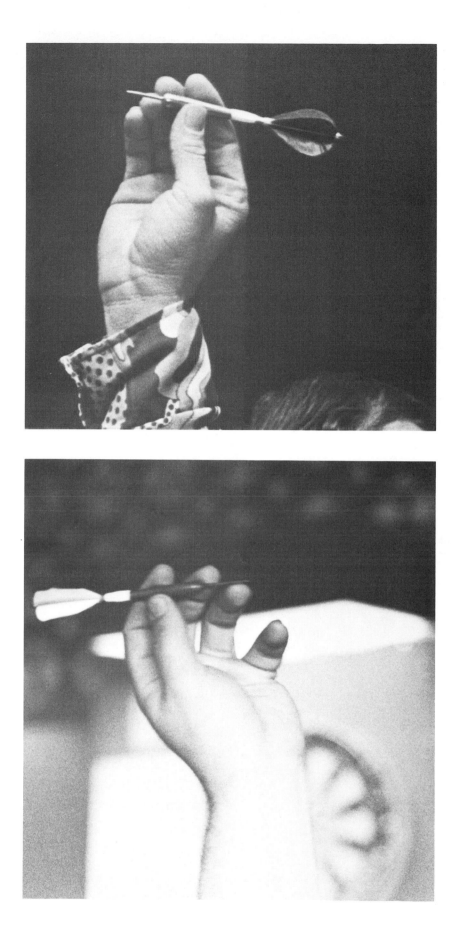

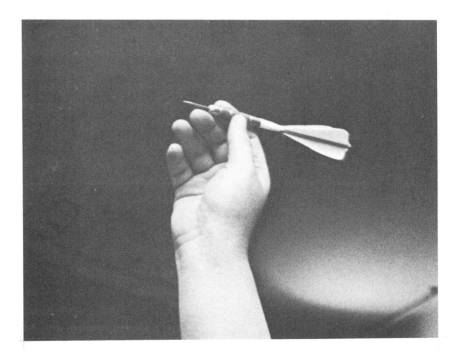

The Stance An improper stance often accounts for the erratic darts that beginners throw. The most important characteristic of a good dart player's stance is natural ease. Stand comfortably with your feet slightly apart. If you are right-handed, the right foot should be slightly ahead of the left, touching the toe line and pointing toward the board. In this position, as the arm sets to throw, the weight falls slightly more onto the right foot than the left. If you are left-handed, the left foot should be forward.

The four basic stances: both feet on the toe line facing the board, one foot on the line facing the board, one foot at a 45-degree angle to the board, and one foot touching and parallel to the line.

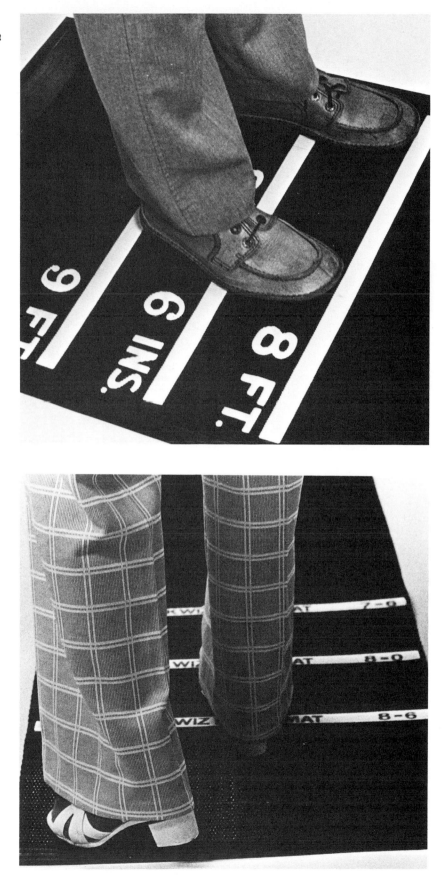

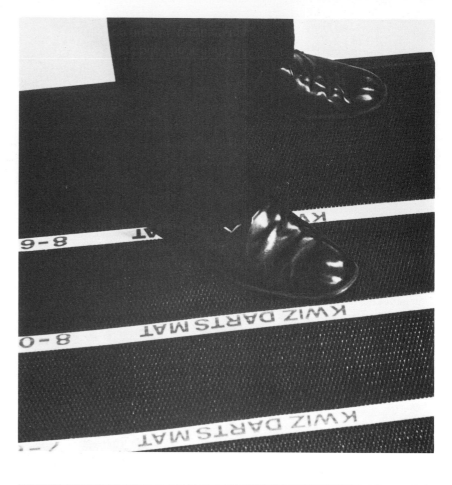

Another good solid stance is to have both feet, spread about nine inches apart, placed on the toe line facing the board.

Some players move about on the toe line to gain a better view of the spot on the board they are aiming for, and the experts often practice throwing from a variety of positions to assure a good sight line. This movement on the toe line is not recommended for the newcomer to darting. It tends to destroy concentration, rhythm, and frame of reference for the next shot. If you feel a particular throw requires you to move, be sure to regain the proper alignment of your stance before the next throw.

Ray Fischer, one of America's top players, throws a dart at the U.S. Open. Note how he positions his front foot against the toe line. The only motion comes from his right arm.

Sighting After you have mastered the fundamentals of holding the dart and have perfected your stance, sighting the dart comes into play. Most good dartists appear to throw without taking aim, but they are actually sighting the dart in the same way as an archer aims his arrows.

To sight correctly, keep your arm close to your body. Using your arm and wrists as pivots with the elbow acting as a fulcrum, bring the dart up and back toward your head. Keeping the dart as close to your line of sight as possible, bring the dart back until it almost brushes your cheek. This lets you throw along your line of sight. Tall players with longer forearms can sometimes get enough force behind the throw bringing the dart back only as far as the face. Try to find a place along the cheek where you find it most comfortable to stop. In doing this you will have a frame of reference after releasing the first dart. A slight, almost unconscious adjustment will bring your second dart into the desired area as long as the starting position for the throw release remains the same. If you bring the dart back in a haphazard fashion, this frame of reference—and the success of your aim—is destroyed.

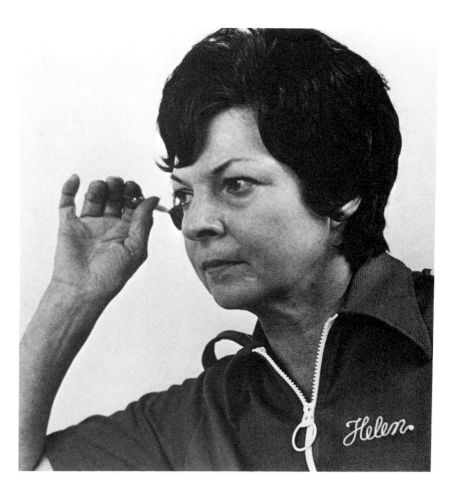

Helen Scheerbaum sights her mark. The dart has been brought back to eye level.

Tony Money keeps his eye on the dart as he finds his line of sight.

Keep in mind that aim in darting is not a "sure thing." You cannot ensure perfect results every time, as you can when shooting a rifle that you have aimed properly. The aim for darts is a reference point from which adjustments are made, often subconsciously to get the dart to the target. In throwing for a double 20, for instance, plan to throw your first dart a bit higher than the scoring area. There are two reasons for this. First, your initial dart usually falls lower than the planned line of flight, which might allow you to hit the double 20 (remember the law of gravity). Second, if your first dart falls near but not in the 20, it will serve as a guide for adjustment as you lower your aim. This works for other numbers and areas of the board as well.

The Throw Although many good players have throwing styles that look unorthodox and even downright unskillful, all these stylized throws have certain fundamental characteristics.

An English player may stand with both feet touching the toe line; Conrad Daniels keeps his right foot touching and parallel to the toe line; Helen Scheerbaum, U.S. women's champion, places her right foot perpendicular to the toe line; and others may place their forward foot at a 45-degree angle to the toe line. During the actual throw, Daniels uses a lot of wrist action while Scheerbaum uses very little. And some players bring the dart back as far as the eye while others bring it all the way back to the ear. The one thing they all have in common is that they never move any part of the body—including their feet—when they throw.

This *anchor concept* is the secret of consistent play. The head must also be kept steady (sound familiar to you golfers?), and you must not jerk the throw. Try to develop a smooth arclike throw using the wrist and elbow as pivots. If you can manage to keep your upper arm parallel to the floor and steady, using only the lower part of the arm and wrist to throw, so much the better. Good wrist action at the moment of release provides extra power for a fast level throw that sticks firmly in the board and stays closest to your line of sighting. Incidentally, the throw need not be *hard,* but it must be *crisp.* The dart should get to the board quickly with as little trajectory as possible; a hard or very strong throw will not accomplish this.

A common fault of the beginner is to forget to follow through on his motion. After you release the dart, simply allow your arm to continue in its natural motion. Just as a baseball pitcher who neglects his follow through has little control, the dartist who abruptly ends his arm motion as he releases his dart will not hit the desired mark. Let your hand, with the fingers fully extended, follow the dart as it moves toward the board. Many players who never advance past "average" fail because they neglect throwing fundamentals.

A common fault of the beginner is to forget the follow-through. After you release your dart, allow your hand, with fingers fully extended, to follow the dart as it moves toward the board.

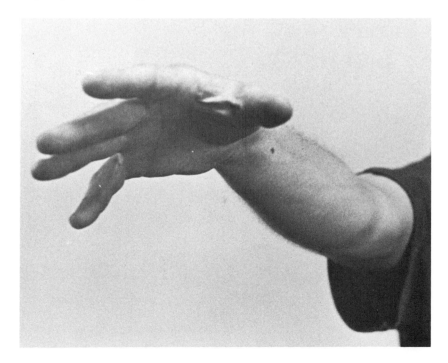

Right

Wrong

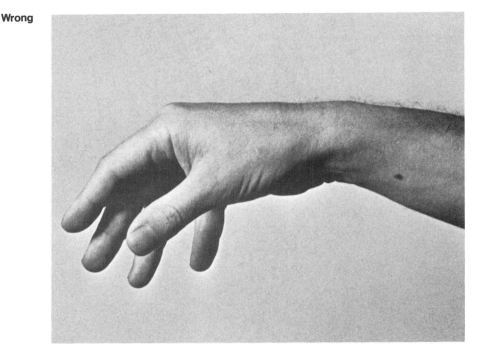

Practice   None of the fundamentals can be a natural part of your game unless
they are practiced. You should set up an organized program of practice so that each step in throwing the dart will blend into a simple fluid
motion. Remember that the stance, grip, and throw need to be molded
into your game as an unthinking, natural adjunct to your concentration
on scoring in the number at hand. The great musician or the great
tennis player achieves his status through regular practice. If you want
to be a great dartist, you must commit yourself to many hours of
practice daily.

Several practice techniques have been developed that will help hone
your talents into a consistent scoring effort.

The concept of grouped darts is very important to everyone's game. To
attain this precision, practice throwing your first dart at a particular
number. Then, no matter where the dart lands on the board, throw the
other two darts at the first dart rather than at the spot you hoped to hit
with your first throw. This exercise will sharpen your ability to score;
the first dart will serve as a frame of reference for those that follow.
Once you have mastered the ability to group your darts, high scores
and more pleasurable playing will follow.

Another useful exercise is to throw around the clock, i.e., to hit each
segment of the board in rotation, with as few darts as possible. You
can measure your progress by keeping a record of the number of darts
necessary to accomplish the task. As your skill improves you should
shift the focus of the exercise to the double or triple zone to improve
your game even further.

Grouping your darts is a good way to practice. After your first dart lands in 19, the other two darts are thrown at the dart rather than the number.

Serious dartists use many other methods of practice. In truth, practice technique is limited only by your imagination. For example, training devices such as the three-number call will strengthen your ability to switch numbers when this is needed for a win. In this exercise, mentally choose three random numbers and throw for them in as fluid a motion as you can. Vary the exercise by throwing at the doubles or triples. In the 01 games, this ability to shift to the number needed to finish the game is extremely important. Rhythm is ruined by hesitation and hence so is the accuracy of the throw. Be sure to practice hitting a single of a number as well as hitting doubles and triples. Many close games are lost when the single number needed to set up a double for an end shot is missed. A missed single could give your opponent another opportunity to throw and possibly beat you by going out during his turn—the turn that making the single would have prevented him from having.

A particularly good form of practice is to play against tough competition. Once you have learned the techniques of good play, the most effective way to improve your game is to compete against someone who plays better than you do. If possible, join an organized league, or start one in your area. There is always a lot of pressure in league games, and playing under pressure is necessary if your game is to advance.

It is not good enough merely to have the principles of a good throw in mind as you practice. These principles must become an integral part of your throw. In many cases, having someone critique your throw will bring to light faults—head movement, body movements, and the like—that you might not be aware of.

As in any sport, there is a great deal of psychology involved in darts. First, you must be able to concentrate under a variety of conditions. The arena that you will play darts in can vary from the quiet of your bedroom to the din of a pub, so it is important that you practice under both peaceful and noisy conditions. If you don't learn to turn off the world around you while you are playing, your dart game will suffer. The concentration required in darts should remove all other thoughts from your mind—this is one extremely beneficial aspect of darts because it enables a person to forget his problems. Many professional people who work under a great deal of pressure have discovered that darts is an excellent way to relax.

You must also have confidence in your own ability. You mustn't let anyone destroy your confidence by psyching you out before or during a game. Once you start to question your own ability, you will find your darts wandering all over the board.

Counting There is a mental side to the game that is extremely important if you are to be a winning player. First, you should have the rules of the game down pat. Mistakes pertaining to the rules can cost you a win at a critical time. These mistakes are absolutely unnecessary. Don't assume anything. At your local golf club, all putts less than two feet may be "gimmies." But if you are playing at another club and out of habit pick up your ball, you will forfeit a hole if their rules say that all putts must be holed out, no matter what their distance. Know the rules under which you are playing!

Counting is the part of darting that separates the top-notch tournament player from the average dartist. During play you must always be in control of your score—from the start of a game, through the mid-game, and especially at the end of the game. Controlling the score is so important because it affects the rhythm and frame of reference in the throw. The arm and eye have a natural ability to make minor adjustments in placing a dart in a following throw if the brain can remember the lines of sight, weight, and distance of the previous throw. Should a pause be necessary between throws, the mind often allows this precalculated data to fade, and the next throw becomes, in fact, a completely new one. If you develop the ability to score quickly—with no pause between your throws—you have an important advantage over your less accomplished opponents. Every dartist of championship caliber knows instantly what numbers he needs to finish a game of 01. For example, if 100 is needed, the triple 20 and the double 20 suggest themselves unhesitatingly.

You should always know what numbers you intend to throw at before you toe the line. For the 01 games, the average player should gear his score in the end game to number 32, which is a double 16, for a win. This is the only number that can be divided by two all the way to double 1. If you miss double 16 but land in single 16, you will be left with 16 points, or double 8, and so on down the line. The percentage is in your favor because you always have "live" darts in reserve. The expert player, however, will gear his score to the double 20; he will get to it sooner and usually feels that any double will do—a double is a double. (In the next chapter, "Let's Think About Winning," there's a more advanced number philosophy.)

You should also avoid throwing at a number when the triple of that number will take you to, or over, your required score. Should this happen in error, two darts are wasted, either of which could have proved to be a winning dart. This unlucky triple throw is not bad luck, just bad darts. For example, most players needing 54 are tempted to throw for single 18, double 18. This tactic seems sound; once the single is attained, a minor adjustment could bring about a double. But the dart thrown for the single may hit the triple bed and render useless two attempts that could produce a win.

Table 1 shows suggested scoring combinations from 170 down. It should be memorized to give you the best chance of winning a game. These are not the only combinations possible; they are merely suggestions to help you develop the combination concept and get you thinking about the formulation of your own best "out" numbers.

Etiquette and Safety Darts is a gentleman's (and gentlewoman's) game. The etiquette guidelines are subtle, and a player who proves to be a bad sport soon becomes unwelcome at most darting establishments. Since darting requires intense concentration, opponents should never try to bother a player while he is throwing. This means no talking or movement within the player's line of vision. And never heckle an opponent. A dart player respects and appreciates another's skills. A match between good players will always be punctuated with banter of "good darts," "tough darts," "hard luck," and the like.

Table 1. WINNING COMBINATIONS
How to Finish 301 with 3 Darts

170 - t20,t20,xB	128 - t20,18,xB	107 - t16,19,x20	80 - t16,x16
167 - t19,t20,xB	128 - t20,t20,x4	107 - t18,17,x18	80 - 16,t8,x20
164 - t19,t19,xB	128 - t20,t12,x16	106 - t20,6,x20	80 - t20,x10
161 - t19,t18,xB	127 - t19,t18,x8	106 - t20,10,x18	79 - t17,x14
161 - t20,t17,xB	126 - t20,t10,x18	105 - t19,8,x20	79 - 17,t10,x16
160 - t20,t20,x20	125 - t19,t20,x4	105 - t19,16,x16	78 - t18,x12
158 - t20,t20,x19	124 - t20,t16,x8	104 - t18,xB	78 - t14,x18
157 - t19,t20,x20	123 - t19,t10,x18	104 - t18,18,x16	77 - t19,x10
156 - t20,t20,x18	122 - t20,t10,x16	104 - t20,4,x20	76 - t20,x8
155 - t19,t20,x19	121 - t19,t16,x8	103 - t19,6,x20	75 - t13,x18
154 - t18,t20,x20	120 - t20,20,x20	103 - t19,10,x18	75 - t17,x12
153 - t19,t20,x18	119 - t19,t10,x16	102 - t20,6,x18	74 - t14,x16
152 - t20,t20,x16	118 - t20,18,x20	102 - t20,10,x16	74 - 14,20,x20
151 - t20,t17,x20	118 - 20,t20,x19	101 - t19,12,x16	73 - t19,x8
151 - t19,t18,x20	117 - t19,20,x20	101 - t16,17,x18	73 - t11,x20
150 - t20,t18,x18	117 - 19,t20,x19	101 - t20,17,x12	72 - t12,x18
149 - t19,t20,x16	116 - t20,16,x20	100 - t20,x20	72 - t20,x6
148 - t20,t16,x20	116 - 20,t20,x18	99 - t19,10,x16	72 - t16,x12
147 - t19,t18,x18	115 - t19,18,x20	98 - t20,x19	71 - t13,x16
147 - t20,t17,x18	115 - 19,t20,x18	98 - t16,xB	70 - t18,x8
146 - t20,t18,x16	114 - t20,18,x18	97 - t19,x20	70 - 18,12,x20
145 - t19,t16,x20	114 - t20,14,x20	96 - t20,x18	69 - t11,x18
145 - t17,t18,x20	114 - 20,t18,x20	95 - t19,x19	69 - t19,x6
144 - t20,t16,x18	114 - t18,20,x20	94 - t18,x20	69 - 19,xB
143 - t19,t18,x16	113 - t19,16,x20	93 - t19,x18	68 - t20,x4
143 - t17,t20,x16	113 - t19,t8,x16	92 - t20,x16	68 - 18,xB
142 - t20,t14,x20	113 - 19,t18,x20	91 - t17,x20	67 - t17,x8
141 - t19,t16,x18	112 - t20,20,x16	90 - t18,x18	67 - 17,xB
140 - t20,t16,x16	112 - t18,t14,x8	89 - t19,x16	66 - t10,x18
139 - t19,t14,x20	112 - 18,t18,x20	88 - t16,x20	65 - t11,x16
138 - t20,t14,x18	111 - t19,18,x18	87 - t17,x18	65 - t19,x4
137 - t19,t16,x16	110 - t20,xB	86 - t18,x16	64 - t20,x2
136 - t20,t20,x8	110 - 20,t18,x18	85 - t15,x20	64 - t16,x8
135 - t19,t14,x18	109 - t19,20,x16	84 - t20,x12	63 - t9,x18
134 - t20,t14,x16	109 - 19,t18,x18	84 - t16,x18	62 - t10,x16
133 - t19,t12,x20	108 - t20,8,x20	84 - 16,t20,x4	61 - t15,x8
132 - t20,t12,x18	108 - t20,16,x16	83 - t17,x16	61 - 15,6,x20
131 - t19,t14,x16	108 - 20,t16,x20	82 - t14,x20	61 - B,x18
130 - t20,t18,x8	107 - t19,xB	81 - t19,x12	61 - t7,x20
129 - t19,t12,x18	107 - t17,16,x20	81 - 19,t10,x16	60 - 20,x20

You should always be ready to throw when your turn comes up. A subtle form of psyching out used by some players is to make the opponent wait, but this is a "bush" tactic and really signifies a minor leaguer. When it's your turn to throw, take the line, organize your thoughts and concentration, and throw all three darts without undo or obviously planned delay. Let your darts remain in the board until your opponent agrees with your score and the score has been marked on the scoreboard. It is somewhat like a game of poker. A poker player would never call a full house to win a hand without showing it to the calling players. Or he wouldn't do it too often, that's for sure.

The number of spectators at dart matches has grown over the past few years. As a spectator you should never interfere with the progress of a match in any way. Spectators should not heckle or coach players during play. Coaching is not allowed in tournament play, and a player could be disqualified because of a spectator's coaching activities. Players also have obligations regarding spectators. As a player you should see to it that your supporters treat your opponent in a fair manner.

Darts is basically a safe sport, but as in any sport, a person can get hurt while playing or viewing a match if they fail to think about safety. Properly handled, a dart is certainly no more dangerous than a knife, baseball bat, hockey stick, or pool cue. But like the other equipment

Before you pull your darts from the board, make sure that your opponent agrees with your score and mark the score on the scoreboard.

used in sports, a dart can be dangerous when used improperly or carelessly.

One should never allow children to play with darts unless they are supervised by an adult (see page 43 for detailed safety rules for children). Spectators and players waiting for their turn to play should not be permitted to sit or stand near a dartboard because it is possible for a dart to bounce from the board and fly uncontrolled for a short distance. And do not immediately lunge to retrieve your darts after your last dart is thrown. It is conceivable that the last dart could hit a wire and rebound toward you. In all cases, take a few basic precautions and let good common sense be your guide.

Some people make a living out of throwing trick darts. They knock cigarettes out of a stooge's mouth with a dart. Or they hit an apple off someone's head, or knock a button from a protruding tongue, or hit small coins held in someone's hand. This type of activity should never be encouraged by the dart player. The USDA is strongly opposed to tricks as an expression of one's prowess. If a professional trickster insists on performing, however, be sure that he has the necessary skills not to injure anyone. The average dart player should concern himself with learning how to play a proper competitive game of darts, not with playing useless tricks.

LET'S THINK ABOUT WINNING: A LESSON FROM THE EXPERTS

VI

Many of us play sports not only for the enjoyment the sport offers but also with the thought that someday we may become good at the sport—maybe even the best. The only way to become expert in any sport is to practice, practice, and practice. There is no shortcut to the top. Once you have perfected the basics, you can start to look for that little extra something that will enable you to become your league or club champion. One way to get some tips on playing good baseball or basketball is to watch the professionals play. In tennis or golf you might seek the advice of a teaching pro. If darts is your game, you should attend the tournaments held in your area so that you can watch the top players in action. If possible, you might also have one of the outstanding players analyze your game.

But before you start thinking about the finer points of the sport, you must master the basics. Bob Thiede, the 1971 U.S. champion, and the first American to have signature model darts named after him, insists that the beginner must get his "stroke" down. Thiede feels that watching an expert can be helpful, but eventually every dartist must develop a style of his own that is comfortable to him. Conrad Daniels, the 1975 U.S. champion, and currently the third-ranked player in the world, insists that the beginner must learn to repeat every part of his game exactly the same way each time he throws. In this way, he feels, the player's game will become grooved and consistent. The one thing that all the top players stress is that the beginner must practice every phase of his game until it comes naturally and can be performed without thinking.

Measuring Your Skill   How do you know when you are a good player? That's a good question. Frankly, until you have a proven track record at the national tournaments, only you will know how good you are. One thing you should not do is measure your game by your best performance ever. Everyone has an absolutely brilliant day on occasion, and if you tell yourself that this is the normal level of your game, you are kidding yourself. And of course you will be unhappy each time you do not play up to that level. Be realistic in your evaluation of how well you play. Incidentally, try to seek competitors who play on about the same level that you do. If you are not a top-notch dartist as yet, you may become discouraged playing against an expert. But always seek out good competition—maybe players who are a bit better than you are. This will tend to keep you on your toes.

Don't be fooled, either, by the game or two you may have won against a top-notch player. The very nature of the game—where perfection is impossible to achieve—allows the weak to overcome the strong occasionally. This is why the top dartists play head-to-head matches against one another that last for more than a few games. The best of 51 games of 301 or 501 is a very popular competition, with the first player to win 26 games the winner.

For 301, a 12-15 dart game is considered very good, and a 6-dart game is perfect. If you can throw a steady diet of 12-15 tournament 301 games along with an occasional 9-dart game, you could very well be a winner. In straight-start 501, a game that takes 18-21 darts is considered very good; 9 darts being the perfect mark. But in championship play, while the early rounds will produce games of 18-21 darts, the finals will produce many 14-18 dart contests. When you play American Cricket, 21 darts is a very good game, but American Cricket does not generate games that can be judged by counted darts. Usually, when two players are throwing exceptionally good darts against each other, subsequent scores will produce points that will make it necessary for the opponent to counterattack. This element of strategy makes a dart count impractical except in practice when you are playing against yourself for stroke development.

The highest score possible for Baseball is 81 runs; an average of 40-45 runs is very good. In one outstanding game on the English board Bob Thiede threw a game of 71 runs against Denis Carey. Thiede had handicapped Carey with two runs per inning for their match, which was played in New York City's Red Blazer Pub.

These marks of proficiency are only guidelines for you as you assess your playing ability. Along with the number of darts it takes to win certain games, you can judge how good you are by evaluating your consistency. How often do you hit the number you are throwing for? And, if you miss, how far off are you? In England a score of 100 or more is called a *ton*, a term that signifies the weight you have placed on your opponent. Ton records are kept as the measure of a player's consistency. It is really academic whether or not the darts score 100, 140 or 180 because all three scores represent darts that were grouped consistently in and around the triple-20 area. Of course there's a great difference between 100 and 180 on the scoreboard, but the skill is really reflected in the tight grouping around the triple-20 area—and there's a bit of luck involved in being able to squeeze the darts into the small area of the higher scores. Keep track of your tons: they are a good barometer for measuring how good you are getting.

What Makes a Top Player?

Most top players will tell you that a great deal of hand-eye coordination is needed to play darts well. They will also say that a player must be able to concentrate hard enough to block all other thoughts from his mind. Beyond these factors, what is it that makes one player great and another just good? We asked a number of leading players why they felt they were among the foremost players, and we'll pass their answers along to you.

Cleveland's Tony Money, the 1976 U.S. champion, feels that a top player "must have the ability to play the game under pressure." Money said, "I am never nervous but I do feel the pressure during a big match." Money feels that his experience and natural ability enable him to cope with the pressure he knows is there.

Javier Gopar, a leading American player from San Bernadino, California, says that a top player has to develop a positive attitude toward the game. When Gopar plays, he never feels that he will lose. He won't allow the slightest negative thought to creep into his mind. Gopar believes that a championship-caliber player must exercise mind control throughout a game. This concept of confidence is seconded by most of the other top players. Joe Baltadonis, the 1972 U.S. champion from Mt. Royal, New Jersey, said, "Top players are confident players. They gain this confidence through experience. Everything they do is done automatically because of this experience they gained over the years." Baltadonis has won many big tournaments with this can-do attitude.

Javier Gopar coolly sizes up a shot.

Joe Baltadonis, the 1972 United States Open champion.

According to Conrad Daniels, the best players have spent a great deal of time thinking about their game and have tried to improve upon it in whatever way they could. Once a certain plateau of proficiency is reached, each little advance after that is a product of hard work—and the results of each succeeding step are minimal. Conrad says, "The smart players sit down and analyze the games of their opponents as well as their own game. A smart player can determine the mental state of his opponent by seeing if the opposing player has changed anything from his normal playing style. If the opponent's game goes bad, and you know it, you have gained a tremendous edge." States Daniels, "I try to make the sport as scientific as possible and to eliminate human error as much as I can."

One of the best women players in the world, Helen Scheerbaum, the reigning U.S. champion from Philadelphia, believes that a top player "never accepts anything but the best. If you go into a tournament hoping for a respectable placing, that is the best you can hope for, and you play to that goal. All players feel a bit of nervousness, but if you're confident you'll be able to handle the jitters with ease."

Ray Fischer, another great player from Philadelphia, thinks that a winning player must have determination. To be a winner you can't enjoy losing. This sense of competitiveness is a necessary ingredient of a champion in any sport. Irish International player Tommy O' Reagan puts this attitude into perspective when he says, "A top player can have no fear of another player."

The experts suggest that you know not only how you game shapes up but also that of your opponents. Practice so much that you believe your game is the best; then try to measure it against another player whenever you can. If you game is not good enough, go back to the dartboard for more practice. Conrad Daniels says the sum total of your game is what all those little advances you make in practice add up to. Keep putting the pieces together, so to speak, and someday you may wear the U.S. champion's crown.

Preparing to Throw

Before you play winning darts, you must have perfected your stance and grip. Consider Daniels' advice that the successful dartist always uses exactly the same stance and grip for each and every throw. By doing this, he feels, a player will know that his game will always be consistent. Every top player consciously checks his feet before throwing. As Tony Money prepares to throw, he looks down at his feet to see that they are properly aligned with the toe line. Joe Baltadonis consciously places his left foot dead center on the toe line (Joe is left-handed) and thinks only about this foot placement.

There are four common stances among the experts. Alan Evans, like many English players, stands with the toes of both feet touching the toe line, making him stand square with the dartboard. When players like Evans throw, they bend slightly forward at the hip and give a slight twist to the lower torso as they release the dart. Helen Scheerbaum places her right foot perpendicular to the toe line with her left foot about nine inches to the rear to stablilize her throw. Her weight is on the right foot, and she pushes off the ball of her left foot for the throw. Conrad Daniels stands with his right foot twisted so as to be parallel with and touching the toe line. His left foot is behind his right, and the toes of his left foot make about a 45-degree angle with the lines. Most American players, however, use this stance: Their forward foot touches the toe line at a 45-degree angle; their back foot rests to the rear, with most of their body's weight centered over the forward foot.

All these stances have one thing in common. Once in place, the forward foot is planted. There is no movement. This is vital for an accurate throw. Daniels believes that the English stance and his style are the best for a very practical reason. "If you use these stances, you can always be sure that your foot placement is correct," he says. He has studied other players that use other methods of foot alignment and has determined that they never place their feet in exactly the same position for every throw. He feels that this is a flaw in their game—and some of them are top players too. Daniels adds, "Your stance is right if you can accomplish what you want every time you throw."

Before any good dartist throws, notice how he fingers the darts to get a good grip. Scheerbaum twists and turns the dart in her hand until the

The Conrad Daniels signature model dart has grooves where Daniels used to place adhesive tape. According to Daniels, a player must always place his two fingers on the same spot on the dart.

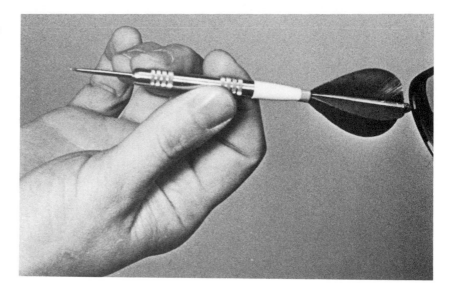

proper feel develops. Daniels is very particular about his grip. He uses two fingers and his thumb, and the thumb is under the balance point of the barrel. Daniels used to place adhesive tape on his darts to assure himself that his fingers were always on the same spot. When the Conrad Daniels signature model was produced, it was manufactured with knurled grooves in exactly the same places that he used to put his tape. Just as a bowler grips the ball before eyeing the pins, Daniels says that a player should secure his grip before taking the line to throw.

"The dart is easier to control if you don't grip it with your fingertips. Move it slightly on your fingers," says Daniels. "If you find that your darts are floating, apply pressure with your thumb and squeeze with more force."

When you play darts on a new court, make some observations before you throw your first dart. Check the lighting for shadows you will have to take into consideration when sighting. And determine if the board's measurements are correct. Many experienced players pace off the distance from the toe line. This careful check of distances is not a criticism of the court but is meant to establish where they should play from on that particular board. You may notice in a pub match that a player is standing an inch or two behind the marked toe line. This is because the player feels that the board might be measured a bit short, and his stroke and eye coordination is geared for the exact 8-foot distance he practices from.

You should also check for wind currents, which can influence the flight of your darts. Scheerbaum used to use the popular Philadelphia tournament wooden dart. She found that the air currents created by fans and air conditioners affected her darts too much so she switched to a brass model. The change gave her darts the stability that made her America's number-one female player. She now has the honor of being the first American woman to have her own signature model dart.

In summary, before you actually make your throw you should make sure that your grip is exactly the way you want it to be; make sure that

Conrad Daniels places his foot along the toe line (*top left*).

Before looking at the board, Daniels checks his grip (*top right*).

Daniels' weight then moves forward onto the front leg (*bottom left*).

Daniels is now ready to shoot. He sights first, then begins his throwing motion (*bottom center*).

Daniels' arm and shoulder are directly in line with the number he is shooting for. This assures an up-and-down arm motion (*bottom right*).

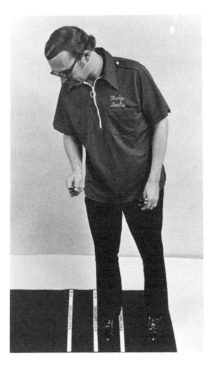

your foot is placed on the line where you want it to be; and make sure that there is a looseness in your stance that will allow your throwing arm a comfortable, free motion toward the board. When all this is done, then, and only then, are you ready to look to the dartboard.

Making the Throw   If your stance and grip are good, the throw will be much easier. Daniels always stands so that his arm and shoulder are directly in line with the number he is throwing for. This assures an up-and-down arm motion instead of a side-to-side arm motion. "Why throw at different numbers with a different motion?" he asks.

When you are ready to throw, pull the dart back to some set position by bending the elbow and then move the dart forward by straightening the elbow. Thiede pulls his dart back to around his chin and releases it when the dart is about a foot away from his face. Many top players bring their darts back toward the eye. Daniels sometimes even brushes his glasses or nose with the feathers of his dart. He likes to see his dart as he lines up his throw. Many championship-caliber players, however, feel that you should not be aware of the dart when you aim and throw. Fischer says that when he sees his dart at any time during the throw, he knows that he is not playing right.

Bob Thiede gets ready to throw. Notice the intense concentration.

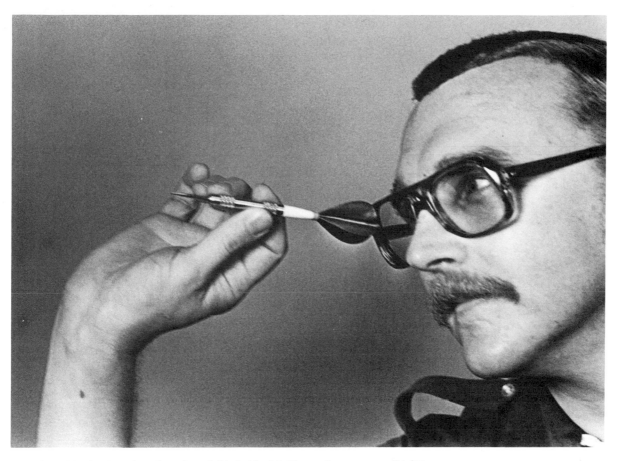

When Conrad Daniels is ready to throw, he pulls his dart back to his eye. As you can see, the dart often hits his glasses.

Most experts look for a tiny spot in the number area they are throwing for and focus on this spot. Baltadonis picks out such a spot and focuses with such intensity that the spot actually grows larger to him. This gives him the sensation of throwing at a much larger target. And his extremely tight groupings, for which he is famous around the circuit, attest to his ability to see these "growing" spots well. Silberzahn explains that when you pick out a spot within a desired zone, even the double and triple zones, your margin of error is the area right around the spot. In this way, you may still hit the scoring area even if you do not hit the spot exactly.

When you throw your dart, your arm guides the dart to the target while your wrist provides much of the thrust. Daniels compares the throwing of a dart with the basketball jump shot. In neither case do you aim at your target, you sort of "feel" it into place. The arm, in particular the elbow and forearm, guide the missile to the target. Daniels' wrist action starts in a bent-back position, similar to that of shooting a basketball. You do not need as much force when throwing this way because the speed of the dart is generated by wrist action rather than arm strength. Consequently, you will be better able to control the direction the dart will take. Players who throw with flat wrists have to throw a lot harder to get the dart to the board.

It is very important that you create some sort of rhythm in your throw. Daniels and Baltadonis both have a short pumping action before they release their darts; Thiede utilizes a rhythmic wrist-twist to establish his tempo. They all feel that you are at a disadvantage if you simply release the dart from the eye position. The principle is similar to the wind-up of a baseball pitcher or the bouncing of a basketball on the floor before the player shoots a foul shot. By developing a motion as you bring back your dart, you will be setting up for its release without interruption. The motion will help gather momentum for the throw.

Think a Little English International player Tony Bell believes that the dart player is the loneliest person in the world when he is competing in front of a crowd—and the larger the crowd, the lonelier he is. One of the big reasons for player nervousness is the fear of not performing up to form. No one wants to look like a turkey. But the top players have learned to turn this apprehensive attitude to their advantage. They try to look calm, cool, and collected even though they may be jumpy and have a stomach full of butterflies. This demeanor can put a tremendous amount of pressure on one's opponent. For this reason, a top dartist can very often play a subpar game and still beat a lower-grade dartist who might be playing the overall better game.

Frank Ennis, a man with a well-earned championship reputation, says that he has had opponents "blow" shots they would normally make because of this unseen pressure. Frank has a reputation of not missing his critical shots. The word on the circuit is not to give Ennis another throw "because he won't miss." Players have been observed packing up their darts after a missed shot even before Ennis stepped to the line for his closing-out throw. This kind of edge is indeed a big one. It all goes back to the idea that you must believe that you can't lose. Don't be swayed from that belief.

Most top players have patterned their games to such a degree that their approach and play come naturally. "If I start thinking, I'm in trouble," says Scheerbaum. "Before I get to the line, I know what I want to throw at and what I'll do if I miss."

The expert tournament player has learned to control his emotions during a game. Most of them pay little or no attention to what their opponents are doing because they are so engrossed in their own play. They have a number philosophy that enables them to decide quickly what to throw for without losing their rhythm. Beginners are happy to hit anything and are quite pleased with obtaining high scores. As you improve you will learn that there are certain numbers, which may not necessarily be the highest scores, that will set you up for your going-out double easier than others. For example, if you had 104 left to make, you could throw for the triple 20, single 12, and double 16, which would give you the desired three-dart out. Remember, always try to go out during your turn because if you don't, your opponent has three darts with which to do the same.

U.S. Women's Champion Helen Scheerbaum shows the style that has made her a consistent winner. The great amount of time she has spent practicing enables her to perform successful throws automatically.

The intermediate player is taught to reduce his score to 32 because from this point the player has five working opportunities to throw at a double should his darts hit the single of the number he needs. A single 16 will still leave double 8, a double 8 will still leave double 4, and so on all the way down to double 1. The number 32 is the only number of the board that will leave a five-time split. The top players, however, more often reduce to double 20 because it is much more available at an earlier part of the game and still gives a good percentage break-down factor of three splits. In any case, the expert reduces his score to the first available double, even if that happens to be the double bulls-eye. You must not let your opponent throw again!

According to Daniels, darts is a sport of percentages. The best players have studied the numbers and worked out all the available combinations. Your number philosophy should be based on statistics and your own particular game. If triple 19 is easy for you, then why develop your number philosophy around triple 20? If you have 72 to make, would you throw for triple 12 (36 points) as most of the charts tell you to do? Daniel says no. The percentages favor your hitting a triple 20 because you throw for it most often, and should you hit it, you will still be left with a two-split double.

For an 82, only a few of the experts won't throw for the double bullseye with their first dart, instead of the "chart popular" triple 14 (42 points). The reason behind this is that if you should hit a single 14, you would still need 68 points. This would in turn require that your next dart be a double or triple to give the one-dart shot at a game-winning double. By throwing at the double bulls-eye first—if you hit, it gives you two darts at double 16—you are likely to hit a single-bulls-eye or possibly a high single number, which will leave you a single to do to place you on a game-winning double. The 82 less the single bull (25) leaves 57, which then allows a single 17 and a double 20. After you reach a certain level of play, you will be amazed at how far you can advance in the sport if you just stop and think about it a bit.

In figuring out the possible combinations for any number, the important thing is to analyze and adjust the combinations to suit your game. Develop your own progressions and learn them so that they come naturally when you are on the line. One example of the "think" process would be setting up one number from the other. For instance, how would you attempt to go out with 126 remaining? (Remember: You must not give your opponent another throw if you can possibly help it.) Triple 19 is the first shot for this one. If you miss the triple and get a single, the next dart should be zeroed in on triple 19 again (for a total 4 x 19, or 76 points). This will leave you with a possible double bullseye for going out. Try to adjust your combinations to make a triple and a single; this leaves one dart for a double, any double. Choose your first triple so that should you miss and hit the single, that score, subtracted from the total, will still let you make another triple, which will place you on a double. Of course, if your opponent hasn't scored yet, or if you are far out in front on points, you might consider jockeying for a desired double instead of pushing for a quick out. Don't forget, however, that your opponent can go out in one turn from 170 points down.

When you know what you must throw at in order to win, your overall concentration is much greater. This helps reduce the tension in a match—your mind is fully occupied with the game. The more you concentrate on the game, the better you'll do. Daniels and Scheerbaum both claim that a bomb wouldn't disturb them when they are playing.

Tossing Brass   No one is naturally good in a sport; everyone has to practice. The expert dart player is no different. He didn't acquire his skill overnight. All his actions while playing are the result of experience, but they become like a sixth sense. Once a dartist reaches the top he finds that he must still practice, maybe more than before. Practice is relative, however. Four or five hours a day might be okay for some players, but this much tossing brass could sour another player's game. Over-practice sometimes causes the "yips" or "colly-wobbles," which are two terms for a psychological phenomenon that affects a player when he tries too hard. When the yips take over, you'll notice a slight hitch in the throw and feel an almost imperceptible tightening of the muscles in your arm. Practice enough to keep your game sharp. If you notice any deterioration, cut back the practice sessions slightly.

Most of the top players play enough to keep their game sharp. But do not confuse four or five hours of pub play with an hour's practice at home by yourself. Golfers spend many hours on the practice tee and putting green to sharpen their game for the few hours that they actually play. When you are playing you cannot work on any particular phase of your game; you will toss ten times as much brass during the shorter time spent practicing.

Gopar practices as much as he can. This might mean a couple of hours on some days and no time on others. He doesn't think that a dartist should play against himself when practicing, and Silberzahn seconds that. They feel that if you play against yourself, you will soon become bored if you are throwing well and disgusted if you are throwing poorly. For his practice, Gopar goes around the board throwing at triples, then doubles. He always tries to group the three darts in each zone. Silberzahn, on the other hand, tries three dart combinations with three darts going in different directions even if he misses the desired triples.

Other championship-caliber players do play against themselves. They feel you have only yourself to beat in a match, as you must know exactly what kind of performance you are capable of. Darts is really an offensive game only. A good offense is the only defense you have. You cannot do anything about your opponent's good darts except throw better back at him.

Tony Money plays twenty games against himself and checks them for consistency. He records the number of darts for each game (he counts every dart, missed ons and missed outs). If he averages 17 darts for 301, he knows he is doing well. He closes out his practice sessions by trying to get a 25 bulls-eye count with 25 darts.

Joe Baltadonis likes to go around the board on the doubles. He measures how sharp he is by recording the number of darts it takes him to do the task. And he practices the cork shot only if he thinks he will need it in a tournament, either for Cricket or when a bulls-eye determines the order of play.

Many top players practice by playing head-to-head matches against each other. When a tournament is nearing, Ray Fischer and Frank Ennis sharpen their game by squaring off against each other. This is not always enough, though. If you are throwing well, matches are fine. But if there is a problem with your game, you must work on that particular problem. If you lose your stroke, rhythm, balance, grip, or some other phase of your game, you should stop and think about what you are doing wrong, then iron it out.

If you're having trouble finding the flaw in your game, ask someone to help you pick it out. Anyone watching you throw will be able to tell you whether you are lunging, moving about on the line, or have developed a hitch in your throw. But if the problem is not quite so obvious, you will have to seek out a better player than yourself for advice.

There is no easy way to become an expert. It takes time and lots of effort. Practice every conceivable shot. The time you spend practicing will definitely pay off for you. Playing well is one sure way to get a great deal of enjoyment from any game.

DARTS AND SCIENCE
VII

For those of you who have become good dart players and might be looking for that extra edge, here's a brief look at the science of darting. This chapter is intended to stimulate your thought processes and bring up a few ideas you may never have considered. Those of you who don't want to get bogged down in cerebral pursuits in a sport that you consider simple can skip this section.

The throwing of a dart can be broken down into three component parts for scientific study. These would be the neuromuscular actions within the body, the science of projectile objects, and the science of optics. Any one part could be further divided, and each subpart could serve as the topic for a doctoral dissertation. We'll just scratch the surface and offer a few thoughts that you might want to pursue further.

Neuromuscular Actions

To throw a dart, a great degree of hand-eye coordination is needed. The brain instructs the muscles of the arm and hand to release the dart in a particular motion so as to hit a tiny target area. Some forty muscles are involved in the throwing of a dart. The slightest aberration by one of these muscles is enough to prevent hitting the target. Although the sport of darting doesn't involve strenuous physical activity, the physiology involved is much the same as for a sport in which a great deal of muscular activity is needed. In part this is due to the amount of nervous excitement caused by competition. When a dartist contemplates his next shot, his heart beats faster and more blood is pumped around his circulatory system. His breathing is more rapid, more oxygen is taken into his lungs, and his muscles tense—the body gets prepared before the exercise actually takes place. Once your muscles start to contract, certain chemical changes occur within your body. The adrenal glands release adrenaline into your bloodstream and speed the body's actions.

The "fuel" needed to supply the energy comes from various body sugars. Some dart players feel that they play best after ingesting a small amount of alcohol. They claim that it steadies them. In reality, a small amount does the opposite: it stimulates. What the alcohol does is serve as an energy source. Alcohol, unlike most substances that are absorbed into the bloodstream, is rapidly absorbed through the stomach and will replenish the "fuel" used up by nervous and muscular exertion. But too much alcohol will eventually serve as a depressant, and will impair your reflexes. The consumption of alcohol while playing darts is not a good idea. H. Keith Brodie, writing for the National Commission on Marijuana and Drug Abuse (*The Effects of Ethyl Alcohol in Men,* March 1973) states that with alcohol consumption, "oculo-motor impairment is largely the result of loss of coordination of the muscles controlling eye movements rather than visual defects, since vision is fairly resistant to alcohol effects." Dr. Brodie further reports that "the effects of alcohol on athletic performance seem to support the traditional restrictions on such beverages before competition." In particular, he observed a diminished accuracy when throwing a ball and shooting at a target with a pistol. It is not difficult to transpose these observations to the throwing of a dart. In the light of these effects of alcohol on performance, the dartist might well consider alternative sources of energy, such as a candy bar.

One should be aware that practice actually serves a physiological need. Any muscular activity is performed with increased efficiency after prolonged practice; in fact, your movements become automatic. This phenomenon is known as *facilitation*. The various nerve pathways traveled by the several messages it takes to throw a dart become better fitted to carry these messages. The particular act, or series of acts, can then be performed with greater precision and ease.

The tournament player should be aware of the importance of physical fitness. Most tournaments are a grueling experience. Play can begin in the morning and continue late into the evening. The successful tournament player must be physically able to stand about waiting to compete or be on call for twelve or more hours in any given day. Clothing should be chosen to allow for maximum comfort. Particular care should be taken in selecting shoes, since dart throwing puts a great deal of strain on the feet and legs. A flat-heel, hard-sole shoe generally produces the least amount of strain. Platform shoes or shoes with high heels not only cause excessive pressure on the front of the feet, but also cause strain on the shoulder of your throwing arm.

Dartists who suffer any injury or feel pain when throwing should examine their throwing technique. Pain in the shoulder area is most common, but an elbow pain similar to "tennis elbow" or hand cramps are also possible. Shoulder pain is usually caused by an unnatural stance and can often be corrected by some adjustment in your stance. Elbow problems may indicate that you are throwing your darts too hard. It is wise to do some simple stretching exercises of the arm and shoulder area before playing darts. Dartists also find that the squeezing of a hard rubber ball for a few minutes each day often reduces the frequency and severity of hand cramps.

Projectile Motion Galileo enlightened us most on the science of throwing an object, some four hundred years ago. When a dart is thrown horizontally, it has a downward acceleration, like any free-falling body, from the moment it leaves the hand. This downward acceleration occurs independently of the forward horizontal motion. The two components of motion do not affect each other. If air resistance is small, a dart thrown horizontally moves with a constant horizontal velocity (zero acceleration) while the downward component of the acceleration is 32 feet per second per second (gravity). The path followed by the dart will be a combination of the two motions, creating a parabola. This accounts for the slight curve along the path of most darts. To eliminate the curve, the dartist must throw the dart with a greater velocity. The general rule is: The higher the speed of the dart, the flatter the trajectory will be. You can calculate the vertical distance your dart will fall, if you know the velocity of your darts, by using the following formula:

$$\text{distance} = \frac{32 \text{ ft. per sec.}^2 \times 64 \text{ ft.}^2}{2 \times \text{velocity}^2}$$

To keep the dart from falling more than an inch, the dartist must throw it with a velocity of 80 miles per hour. But since most players have an arc in their throw, the average player probably throws the dart at less than half that speed. By the way, this is the one area in which a taller player has an advantage. The taller player is throwing down at the board and therefore does not have to be concerned with arc as much as a shorter player.

This speed is hard to believe, but because a dart is so light in weight, it does not take much force to create a high velocity over a distance as short as eight feet. Our calculations neglect any drag caused by air resistance, however. Because the dart weighs so little, air resistance can be a factor. Air resistance depends on the density of the air or, in

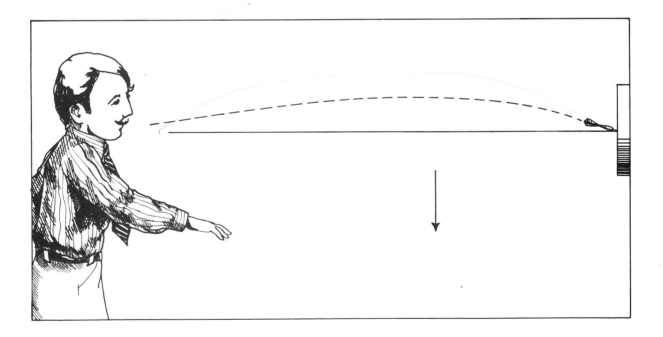

simpler terms, the air pressure. Air pressure is the weight that the air exerts on an object. Normal air pressure is about 15 pounds per square inch. This pressure varies with temperature and humidity. The hotter and/or more moist the air, the less the air pressure will be. The dart player should be aware that as air pressure changes, the trajectory of his darts will change. The greater the air pressure, the harder and faster you must throw your darts. This is especially important if you are playing for a long time and conditions in the room change. As the crowd gets larger, the room temperature will increase, causing the air pressure to decrease. This enables you to decrease the velocity of your darts. If there is a lot of smoke in the room, the air pressure could increase. This means you must throw the dart harder or faster.

One reason why many dartists prefer to throw heavier darts is that they appear to have a flatter trajectory. This is because they are not affected much by air resistance. One must consider, however, the additional force that must be supplied when throwing the heavier dart. It is possible for this extra force to cause muscle fatigue, especially near the end of a long, hard tournament day. Obviously, fatigue will result in a diminishment of accuracy.

The basic shape of a dart has always remained the same. Someday, someone might consider Bernoulli's principle and design a better dart. Basically, his principle says that when the speed of the air increases at a particular point, the air pressure at that point will decrease, which will in turn create lift. There probably hasn't been any research as to what shape a dart really ought to be. And flights, too, could probably be designed so as to offer more lift for the dart. This would involve constructing flights in a shape similar to an airplane wing, which would in turn require new techniques for throwing them at the board.

Optics   Finally, the dart player ought to ponder the science of optics. Your eyesight must be sharp to achieve maximum efficiency for your darts. One eye defect that you may not even be aware and that could hinder your game is astigmatism. This prevents the eye from forming distinct images and could keep you from focusing properly on your mark. Many people who have otherwise excellent vision are astigmatic. The lighting around the board could also affect your darts. Your eyes are receptors of light stimulation, and any light that enters your eye will be recorded by the brain. In setting up the dart court it is important to provide good lighting, and care must be taken to make the background around the board either a dark color or dull black. Light must not bounce off the background. When it does it establishes a contradiction of sight; the pupil of the eye is trying to focus on a spot on the board and at the same time the excess light causes the pupil to constrict. Dartboard manufacturers of the future might even consider changing the colors on the board. Generally, light colors reflect light better than dark ones, so the red and black colors on the board do not offer the best targets.

If you stare at the dartboard and then quickly close your eyes, you will still see your target on the "back of your eyelids." This phenomenon is called *persistence of vision.* The impression made upon the retina of the eye by a given picture persists for about one-sixteenth of a second after the picture has been removed. This is a good reason for developing a rhythm to your darts. If you throw your second dart shortly after your first one, your brain will still carry the "picture" of your first shot and be able to compensate for any deficiencies in it.

But, despite any possible scientific data that one might use to improve his game, darts is not a complicated sport. This section was included to make darts more interesting and intriguing, but don't take it so seriously that it spoils your fun. After all, darts is a sport. It should be enjoyable, not a chore.

TOURNAMENT
DARTS
VIII

For months, you've been practicing for many hours every day. And you've taken on all your friends with a great degree of success. Maybe you've joined an organized darting league. But you're still curious. How good a player am I? How do I measure up against other players from other areas? Once you start asking yourself these questions, you are ready to enter a tournament. The pressure at a tournament serves to separate the very good dart player from the average dartist.

There is nothing quite like the thrill of winning a few matches in one of the big tournaments. And when you play in a national tournament, you might have an opportunity to test your skill against a champion like Tony Money, Conrad Daniels, or Helen Scheerbaum. Just the chance to see these great players in action would make the time and effort of attending a tournament worthwhile. To play against them could do wonders for your own game—and *you* could be the one that knocks them out of the tournament.

Types of Tournaments Tournaments can be simple events with only a few players entered that run for a couple of hours, or they can be elaborate affairs with hundreds of participants that stretch over a number of days. Let's take a look at some of the various types of tournaments and explore the possibilities of conducting one yourself.

Club or Pub Tournament A sport club or pub where darts is played often holds a tournament for its patrons. These tournaments usually draw only a few players and are run in a limited amount of time. The game played is usually the local favorite. There may be no prizes or there may be a few small gifts and trophies, but you'll always find good competition and good fellowship. For these tournaments, each player's name is written on a piece of paper, then placed in a container. Names are drawn "out of the hat" (see details on how to conduct the draw on pages 116-118). The winners of the first round move on to the second, and so on, until only one player remains, the winner.

A group of clubs and pubs often conducts an ongoing competition that determines the best player in the area. These are called Up the Ladder or Up the Stairs tournaments. For a tournament of this type, a list of players is prepared, ranking players from best to worst. This can be a loose ranking so don't despair if you are not placed as high in the ladder as you think you ought to be. You'll have a chance to correct any initial seeding mistakes; besides, this is the ladder's function.

After the ranking is done, the names are listed, hung perhaps on tags or another movable type of label, with the best player's name at the top of the list and the worst player at the bottom. Any player one or two positions below another player can challenge that player for his position in the ladder. If the challenger wins, the challenger and the defeated player swap places. If the challenged player wins, he retains his position. Moving up can be accomplished only by winning; moving down, by losing. There is one exception to this. Some sort of defending schedule must be established, say, a match-a-week minimum. If a challenge is not met, the change of position takes place automatically. This eliminates players from holding on to their high positions on the ladder through inactivity.

League Tournaments

Most of the dart leagues conduct some sort of tournament to select the league's best player. This tournament is usually not part of actual league play. Some leagues run an open tournament, which permits all the league's players to enter. Others let each team conduct a playoff to select their representative, and each team representative plays against other team representatives for the title. Some leagues determine a champion by having a playoff among the members of their all-star team only. Regardless, league tournaments are open for play to league members only.

Local Tournaments

Local tournaments are usually produced by the leading league in an area. These tournaments are open to any player who wants to compete. The players in a local tournament do not have to be a registered member of any particular league. The tournaments are usually multi-event contests with small purses or prizes and appeal to players who live within a few hours' travel time of the tournament site. These local events are tremendous tune-up contests to keep your game in top form. All the top players from the area usually attend these tournaments, but it is unlikely that top players from faraway locales will compete.

National Tournaments

A number of tournaments take place during the year that are classified as national events. The prize money for these tournaments may be as high as $30,000. The national tournaments, like the USDA's U.S. Open, draw hundreds of players from all over the country. At these events you will see all of the nation's top players. The competition is so keen that it is almost unbelievable; so many players have developed their game to a high degree of proficiency.

These national tournaments are not just for the players. Of course, if your game is good enough, you should enter as a contestant, but even if you don't intend to play, you should attend as many of these big events as possible. Seeing the experts play will go a long way in

The scene is set for the U.S. Open finals. Playing on a raised stage makes it easier for spectators to view the matches. In addition, the electronic scoreboard, seen at the far right, enables spectators to see instantly what the contestants have hit on the smaller board.

At a large tournament, such as the U.S. Open, a number of boards are in use at the same time. You must also provide an area for spectator viewing.

helping your own game advance. If you would like to receive information about the national tournaments, write to the United States Darting Association, 516 Fifth Avenue, New York, N.Y. 10036.

International Tournaments

A number of tournaments are now worldwide in scope. You earn a place in these tournaments only by invitation or through winning a national playoff. The annual *News of the World* Championship, which is held in London each spring, is recognized as the world championship of darts. The best players in England, Wales, Scotland, and Ireland earn their place in the finals through elimination play that starts out in the local pubs. The USDA sends the winner of their U.S. Open as America's only representative to this important event. Sweden sends its national champion also. The finals of this championship, which are played in London's Alexandra Palace, draw more than 17,000 spectators and are seen on national television by more than 5 million English viewers.

England televises many other tournaments, such as the Masters and Champion of Champions events. The best selected players from all over the world compete in the heads-on matches in these tournaments.

All international championships offer an excellent opportunity to see world-class darts play. It might be impractical for you to travel to a foreign country just to see a dart contest, but it certainly would be in order to plan any trip you are taking around an international championship time. The feeling at the *News of the World* contest is absolutely indescribable. The excitement created by each dart thrown passes through the crowd like an electrical impulse. It is an experience not soon forgotten.

Running a Tournament

There is probably no one right way to conduct a tournament. Just be sure that the tournament is conducted honestly and efficiently. The mechanics of a tournament can be broken down into several parts, and each part can be executed in many different ways. The end result will always be the same; a champion will be determined.

Selecting a Playing Site

To select the proper place for your tournament, you must have some idea of how many participants you will have. There are problems if the hall is too small; and there are problems, of a different nature, if the hall is too large. In choosing your playing site you should allow enough space to place all the boards you intend to use and still have ample room for spectators.

There should be enough dart courts so that you can maintain a steady flow of play. You want to avoid having players inactive for too long a

Everything is ready for the U.S. Open finals. The finals are held on stage, and seating has been provided for spectators. The trophies for the finalists are on display.

period of time. For the opening rounds in a major tournament, one with about 400—500 contestants, you will need about 32 boards to play on. There are two things to keep in mind about the number of boards. First, although it might seem that the more boards the merrier, this is not the case. There's a point of diminishing return on the utilization of the boards that comes with about 30—35 boards. Play traffic cannot be controlled when you have too many boards. Second, practice boards are nice to have. But unless enough of them can be put into play, say about one-half the number of actual tournament play boards, there probably shouldn't be any practice boards. When only a few practice boards are available, only a few of the players will actually get any advantage from them. In some cases the practice boards end up being used for impromptu matches, and the boards are hogged by a few players. These few then have an unfair advantage because they have warmed up for the tournament matches while other contestants have not. Whatever the playing conditions, an active effort must be made to keep the conditions the same for everyone.

Each board must be properly illuminated and have a scoreboard visible to the players. Each board must stand on its own, without other boards backing or attached to it, so that movement and play on other courts will have no effect (e.g., moving backboards when a player is trying to focus his eyes for a shot). And you should plan to play your final matches on a stage or some sort of elevated platform so that spectators can enjoy the finals to their fullest.

Registration   You must have a method for registering contestants before the tournament begins if it is a major tournament. This is the only way to determine the number of players that will be in each event and, equally important, to determine if any player may inadvertently have registered twice. With preregistration, usually by mail, the tournament director has the number of players to work with and the registration officials are able to check with incoming players to make certain that all who registered are included in the draw.

Keep in mind that when a posted time for starting an event comes, the event must start. It is extremely unfair for players who have registered on time to have to wait for late registrants who are lined up to register at the tournament site.

Registration can be done on the spot and work effectively for tournaments that are not too large. There must be enough people to help with the registration to get the players signed up quickly. Cut-off time must

An area away from the playing courts should be set aside for registration verification.

Trophies and checks should be awarded immediately after the finals of each event. Here the members of a victorious four-person team show their winnings.

leave adequate time for the tournament director to make a player count, do the draw, and start the tournament on schedule. There must be an absolute cut-off time for this type of registration or the tournament will run long, again at the expense of players who abided by the rules.

Prizes   The type of awards for a tournament varies greatly. Some tournaments simply give trophies or medals to the winners, others solicit prizes from local merchants, still others give cash prizes. Tournaments that offer prize money derive it from two sources: money from entry fees and sponsorship from private businesses. Most tournament organizers use a combination of both sources, although it is possible to have a successful tournament using only one source of revenue. In either case, careful planning is necessary when establishing the tournament's budget. To set the purse structure for a multi-event tournament, the total amount of prize money available should be divided equitably among the various events. To do this, remember to take into account the entry fees and the number of participants in each event. An event that has an entry fee of $10 and 200 players should offer more prize money than one in which the entry fee is $5 and draws only 50 participants.

Overall Finances   The most common error made in tournament production is the failure to take into account overhead expenses. It costs a great deal of money

U.S. Open Champion Tony Money receives his trophy and a check. It adds a nice touch to a tournament when you have an awards ceremony.

to produce a tournament. Your league or organization must rent a suitable hall, publicize the event, and design and print posters, entry forms, and a program. There are also administrative and janitorial services to take into consideration. Obvious expenses, such as dartboards, backboards, and lighting, are usually considered in the pre-planning sessions, but those that are not so evident are often treated too lightly.

Make up a budget and figure out where the funds are to come from long before the first entry fee is collected. Your group, league, or organization must be prepared to sustain any loss or deficit. Hopefully, the tournament will make a profit for the sponsoring organization, but tournaments are not always that predictable. Properly handled, they are a great deal of fun, and a lot of satisfaction can be gained by being on the production end of a successful tournament. Competition is the heart of darting, and a tournament is the most important form of competition.

Games and Events   The open singles event at most tournaments is either 301 with double start and double finish, or 501 with straight start and double finish. 501 is used for most championships and is the game played in the *News of the World* Championship. In addition to singles competition, most tournaments have team events scheduled. Play usually takes place over a weekend so that players with a distance to travel have an opportunity to attend. Serious play commences on Saturday morning and continues through the day and into Sunday for the finals. On the Friday evening before a major tournament, there is often a general open-house-type social with a mixed or luck-of-the-draw doubles event. If need be, late registrations can be accepted at this time.

Team events can take place with four-, five-, or six-person teams. Using an odd number such as five or seven for your team event creates a bit of a problem if there is to be a two-person team event in the tournament. The extra/odd player will have to compete against his doubles partner, who might be a member of another team. Usually teams are made up of two or three doubles teams who stand as a unit rather than as an oddball. Should your tournament be "teams only," any number of players on a team is satisfactory.

A good team game is either 601 or 801. For doubles, an 01 game or American Cricket makes for exciting competition. You might consider a "women only" event. Remember, however, that all other events should be open to both men and women; in time, it is hoped that the need for events restricted to women will disappear. It is demeaning to women players to segregate them into a group that is considered "not quite as good" as the open competition. After all, darts is the one sport that can be played equally well by men and by women, and women should certainly try for the larger purses of the open events.

Be sure to plan your playing time adequately. Oftentimes the pre-tournament planning sessions fail to include an analysis of the number of games to be played during the tournament, or the logistics of people moving about the playing floor. Things to consider are the general level of proficiency of the contestants, the amount of moving space other than the actual playing area, and the number of boards being used. For a high-proficiency tournament you should allow four matches per board per hour for either 301 or 501; allow three matches per board per hour if the caliber of play is a bit weaker. For Cricket, allow three matches per hour; 601, three matches per hour; 801, 2.75 matches per hour. All these estimates are for best two out of three matches. If the tournament is to be best of five, you have to adjust the time accordingly.

By carefully planning the timetable for your tournament's play, you will be able to pinpoint the start and end of the events. Don't worry if some matches take longer than the allotted time because you will have many matches that will finish sooner than you thought. These things tend to balance out. Incidentally, always consider invoking a time-limit rule for each game, say, ten minutes per game. The reason for this is that in a luck-of-a-draw tournament, it is possible to have two raw beginners play each other. Should both these players become stuck on double 1, they could spend hours throwing at this elusive double. This type of holdup is not fair to the other players. A judge should be called into the picture, time the play from the point the holdup was brought to the official's attention, and declare high score or a turn at bulls-eyes to be the deciding factor in the game.

Method of Play There are many ways of conducting a tournament. You could use a one-draw, single-elimination method; a double-loss elimination method; or a round-robin type of elimination where every player plays every other player.

The single-elimination tournament is the fairest way to produce a champion from among a large group of players, and it is the method used to produce champions in all other sports. For this type of competition, a player must continue to win to remain in the event. Once he loses, he is out.

When conducting the single-elimination event, all the participants' names are placed in the "hat." The names are then drawn and placed,

The tournament play profile should be set up in such a way that all participants have an opportunity to see it.

in exactly the sequence that they are drawn, on a tournament profile sheet. At USDA tournaments, self-stick labels with the players' names on them are drawn and posted on the spot in the appropriate place in the tournament play profile.

To set up the profile, it is critical that you know exactly how many participants you will have in the event. Be sure you understand the following discussion completely, or you will not end up with two finalists. You cannot conduct a draw by simply having an even number of players. You start with the number 2 and work with a power of 2 until you reach the working figure that is closest to the number of participants in the event. Powers of 2 are 2, 4, 8, 16, 32, 64, 128, 256, 512, and so on up the line. Once you have the closest power of 2 to the number of players in the event, you must then establish either a Negative or a Positive Tournament Profile.

Negative Profile   You will use a Negative Profile when you have *fewer* players than the power of 2 number you are using. The difference between the actual number of players and the number you are using is made up by inserting "byes" into the tournament profile.

Example: If you have 121 players signed up, you should be using the closest available power of 2, or 128. In the playing profile brackets, you must insert 7 byes before you start your draw. The byes should be

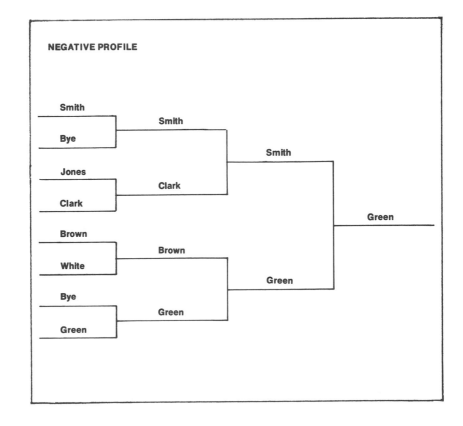

For a Negative Profile, let's assume that there are six players. We use a bracket with eight slots and fill in the two extra slots with a bye. Notice the deployment of the byes.

inserted so that they are spread out a bit and not concentrated in the first few segments of eight brackets. You then proceed with the draw, putting no names on those lines where byes were established. The players who receive byes automatically make it to the next round. All byes must be effected in the first round of play.

Positive Profile   You will use a Positive Profile when you have *more* players than the power of 2 number you are using. In this case, there will be no byes; rather, a number of players will have to play an extra round to participate in the major bracket. The number of players over the number you are using should be doubled to determine the number of players who will have to play the extra round.

Example: If you have 271 players, you should use the number 256, which is the power of 2 closest to the number of entrants. You have 15 players more than the number of playing spots. This means that 30 players have to play one more match than the rest of the players in the event. In effect, it could be said that all the players who do not have to play an extra match received a bye, but whether it is termed byes or an extra round, the procedure for establishing your working bracket is the same. Again, these extra matches should be spread out in the bracket so that they are not all bunched up in any playing segment. These extra games are the first games to be played for the event.

In setting up your profile there is much to be said for "seeding" the best players. When you seed players, you rank them according to their ability. Balance of profile strength is what is most important in seeding. Seeding ensures that the top and bottom half of your profile brackets will be relatively equal in playing strength. You normally seed only the top 8 or 16 players, although you can rank as many as you want. The names of the seeded players are placed on the profile sheet before the draw. The names are entered in such a way that the number-one seed and number-four seed share the same half of the bracket, while numbers two and three share the other half. The breakdown for placement of the other seeds is made with the same sort of consideration. One to be at the top, four to be at the bottom of the same basic half of the overall bracket. While three is seeded at the top of the lower half of the overall bracket, two would be at the bottom. This kind of division spreads out the good players and ensure that the finalists in each half of the bracket are previously tested players, or new players who had to beat top seeds to get to the top spot. This produces a quality champion for your tournament.

If byes are to be given, seeded players often receive them, but this does not have to be the case.

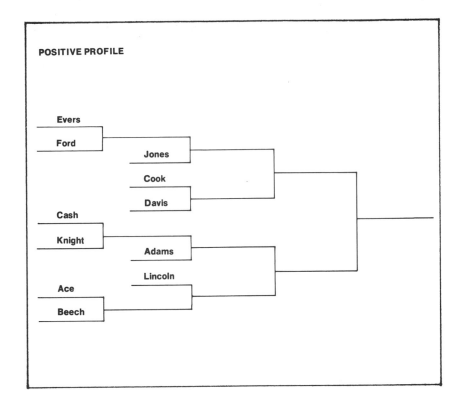

POSITIVE PROFILE

Evers
Ford
Jones
Cook
Davis
Cash
Knight
Adams
Lincoln
Ace
Beech

For a Positive Profile, let's assume that there are eleven players. We again would use the bracket with eight slots—8 is the nearest power of 2 to 11. Six players would play for the three available slots. After the first round, the profile would reduce in the same way as a fully manned profile.

The Flow of Play

The slower the pace of the tournament, the more disgruntled the players. The tournament director must keep the play moving at a rapid pace. He must use all available boards to their utmost. To do this, a command post should be established away from the actual area of play. The director must keep track of the progress of each game as well as the use of the dartboards. Using match-report sheets helps make this task easier.

When players are called for their match, they receive a report sheet with the names of both participants/teams on it and the board assignment for the match. At the conclusion of the match, they return the sheet to the director with the match score entered. The director then knows the result of the match and the fact that a board is free of play and ready to be reassigned.

The tournament director is also responsible for maintaining the tournament profile. With this kind of control, a skillful director can run a number of events simultaneously. There is no reason why you cannot run a number of events at the same time, but you must be careful not to call players for an event if they are still playing in another match that is running concurrently.

Tournament Officials

The executive committee for the tournament can be subdivided into various committees, each handling a specific duty, e.g., publicity com-

The tournament director needs a command post from which to direct play. He also must have a
public address system to keep the players informed.

mittee, registration committee, trophy committee, and the like. Nevertheless, there must be one person designated as Tournament Chairman, or Director, who will assume complete control over everything that takes place. In the planning stages, and during the actual tournament, many things come up that will need to be resolved immediately. Somebody must have the authority to get things done.

The actual tournament requires a minimum number of officials. There should be one general overseer and coordinator of all tournament functions, and another person to direct and coordinate actual play. Under the guidance of these two individuals, properly deployed personnel such as registration coordinators, equipment erectors, and traffic cops will result in a smooth-running tournament.

A panel of judges who might be called upon to make on-the-spot resolutions of disputes should also be appointed. Incidentally, all disputes must be resolved immediately. Complaints about infractions that occurred in past games cannot be honored.

Scorekeepers should not be designated tournament officials. For each match the players should mutually agree on a scorekeeper, usually a volunteer from among the spectators. Even for the finals, when score-

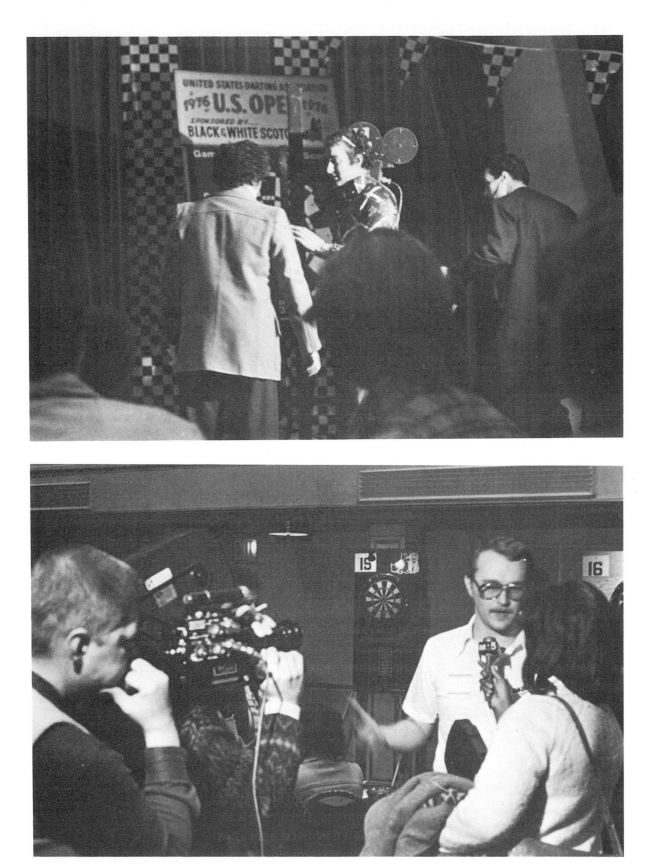

The tournament committee should encourage the media to cover its event. With greater media coverage, more people will become familiar with the sport.

It is a good idea to have dart equipment available at your tournament. You never know when something will break.

keepers are usually appointed, the players must be held accountable for the mathematics of their game.

Spectators   Encourage spectators to attend your tournament. Most players love to play before an audience, and very often, the larger the crowd, the better the games that are played. Make sure that the viewing area is cordoned off from the playing area, so the players are not bothered by undo spectator activity.

Miscellany   *A tournament program* adds a professional touch and is another method of raising funds for the tournament, as advertising space can be sold. The program is also an ideal way to document any special rules that might prevail for the tournament.

A dart retail store is necessary at a tournament and is something the participants will be looking for. Broken shafts and flights will have to be replaced. Also, many players live where equipment is not readily available, and a dart store affords an opportunity to see the latest equipment. A dart store is also another good way to raise revenue for your tournament fund.

Publicity possibilities are tremendous at a dart tournament. And, of course it makes it an extra added attraction for the players if they are playing with the local TV cameras grinding away. Your local newspapers and radio stations will also be pleased to hear about your tournament, and quite possibly will give it extensive coverage.

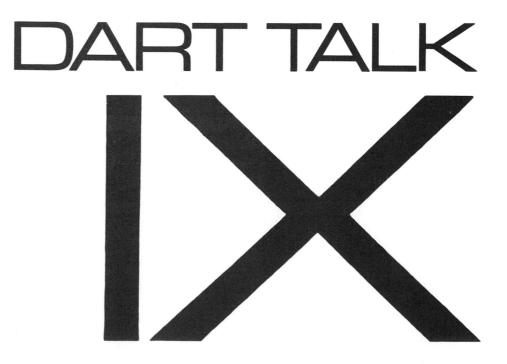

DART TALK
IX

The darting community uses a language all its own, and much of it is colorful indeed. Most of this dart terminology comes from Cockney rhyming slang and is used by dartists throughout the world. The phrases that follow should be a part of your vocabulary before you attempt to hit the big time in darts.

Away This means that you have scored the necessary double to start counting your score. Same as DOUBLE IN.

Bed and Breakfast A score of 26. It comes from 2 shillings 6 pence, the traditional price of lodging, with breakfast, quite a few years ago. Bed and breakfast is not a desired score, but since the darts are most often thrown for the 20 and often drift to the 5 and 1 in the process, it is a common score.

Bed and Breakfast is a 20, a 5, and a 1. If you are shooting for 20s, a miss to either side could give you this combination.

Brush The same as SKUNKED. Try not to get one.

Bunghole Sometimes used to refer to the bulls-eye. Evidently, when the early dartists were throwing at the butt ends of wine casks, the bunghole was the area for a special shot. The bung is the stopper for the hole in which the cask is filled and emptied, so the term bunghole came to mean the hole in the cask.

Bust Busting is getting more points than needed to win the game. In the 01 games, a player can end the game only by getting a double that, when subtracted from his score, leaves him with zero. If subtracting your score leaves you with 1 or with a number less than zero, you have busted. Your score reverts back to what you had before your turn began.

Chalker This is the scorekeeper, and he is so titled because most scoreboards in English pubs are blackboards. In a pub, the next man up in the list of challengers assumes the chalk for the game that determines his opponent.

Clickety-click Score of 66.

Cork, or Bull The bulls-eye, or center, of the dartboard.

Diddle for the Middle To start a game players often throw at the bulls-eye to determine the order of play. When you diddle for the middle, the player throwing closest to the middle gets his choice of when he wants to throw in the order.

Dinky-doo Rhymes with and refers to a score of 22.

Dosser Another of the many terms for bulls-eye.

Double In Same as AWAY.

Double Out To end any of the 01 games you must hit a double that reduces your score to zero. When you double out, you have ended and won your game.

Double Top The number 20 is at the very top of the dartboard, thus a double top is a double 20.

Downstairs The bottom section of the dartboard, which includes 7, 19, 3, 17, and 2.

Feathers A score of 33.

Game Shot The dart that wins the game. When a caller is used at major tournament games, he usually signifies loud and clear—and with quite a bit of emotion—"game shot," as soon as the winning double is scored. The crowd awaits this spirited call.

Garden Gate Another rhyme, it means a score of 88.

Heavy Darts This does not refer to the weight of your darts. It is a compliment on your high score for the turn.

Hockey This refers to a raised toe line from which a player throws. It often is used to simply signify the toe line whether it is raised or not.

Kelly's Eye Double 1. This is the least desirable double to throw for because any miss on the board results in a bust.

Local The local is your favorite pub or tavern where darts is part of the pub's activities.

Madhouse Double 1. This term especially pertains to the situation in which both players need a double 1 to win.

madhouse

Perhaps not being able to hit the double 1 drove these players to their madhouse.

Mugs Away The "mug" is the loser of the previous game. Away is an invitation to the loser of a previous game to throw first in the next game.

Nice Darts, or Good Darts A compliment from your opponent. Since sportsmanship is an integral part of darting, you will hear this often at a dart match.

On Your Knees Since knees rhymes with threes, this is a score of two 3s.

Pug Another of the almost endless terms for the bulls-eye.

Shanghai This occurs when a single, double, and triple of the same number are hit during a single turn and results in an automatic win. When this happens against you, you've been "shanghaied."

Skunked Just about the worst thing that can happen to a dart player. It means that your opponent beat you before you even doubled in.

Three in a Bed It has nothing to do with a nap, quite the opposite actually. Three in a bed is the ultimate shot in dart playing. It means that you have thrown all three darts of a turn into the same triple or double zone. Especially prized are three triple 20s for a score of 180, and three double bulls-eyes, for a score of 150.

Tin Hat The Same as SKUNKED. Try hard not to wear one.

Ton A score of 100.

When is a ton not 2,000 pounds? When you are playing darts and you score 100 points in a turn you have hit a ton.

shooting a ton

Tough Darts This is another expression of good sportsmanship. Your opponent is telling you what bad luck you had when your dart missed its mark. Often said when a dart kisses off another or when a dart's score is lost by hitting a wire and bouncing from the board.

Unfortunates Away Same as MUGS AWAY.

Up in Annie's Room Another term for the dreaded double 1.

Upstairs The top section of the dartboard, which includes 12, 5, 20, 1 and 18.

Wet Feet When a part of your foot is over the toe line, you've got wet feet.

Whitewash Same as SKUNKED.

Getting your feet wet won't always give you a cold, but it certainly will produce an angry outcry from your opponent.

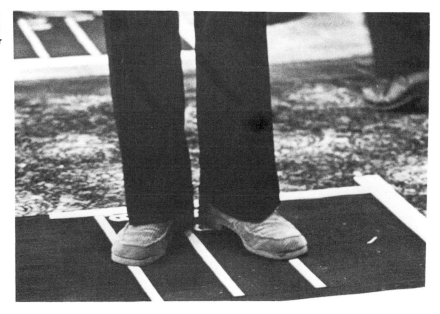

ORGANIZATIONS AND LEAGUES

X

In the United States there are many local dart leagues that offer dart players an opportunity to compete in organized play. At the end of this chapter you will find a list of the leagues that are already in existence in the States.

If you become serious about darting, you should consider joining a dart league. The regular competition against your friends, in formal league play, will give you an opportunity to perfect your game. It will also add a new dimension of pleasure to the sport for you. Quite possibly you live in a city where darts is already being played and a league is in session; if so, you should consider joining in on the fun. If there isn't a league in your town, why not start one?

Your league can be as formal or informal as you want it to be. It takes only about twenty players to get something going. Naturally, the more players you have, the more services and league activity you will be able to generate. The Southern California Darts Association has more than 3,000 members; they play almost every night of the week and operate autonomous singles, teams, and mixed teams leagues. In Washington, D.C., the Washington Area Darting Association has more than 2,000 members, and they offer their members multi-night activity. New York City's Knickerbocker Darts has about 1,000 members and plays on Tuesday evenings. As you can see, your league can develop any sort of format that will satisfy your peers.

Starting a new league may sound like a difficult task. But if you make your plans carefully, and make them easy to carry out, starting a league can be outright fun. Of course, it takes hard work and a lot of cooperation at first. The administration and paperwork have to be rotated among willing members. As the league grows, you might consider paying the administrators and functioning in a more businesslike manner.

You can make your league as formal as your group would like. Some leagues have intricate constitutions while others have all their regulations set down on a few pieces of paper. Whichever way you choose, the following suggestions are offered to help you organize your thoughts about the league's formation.

First, sit down and write out a set of league guidelines. These would include such items as objectives, membership, officers, elections, meetings, and so forth. In other words, decide what type of organization yours will be. You should also figure out a method for raising operating funds. In order for your league to be a functional organization, you will have to collect some form of dues. These can be assessed to the members or solicited from team sponsors.

Once you have the basic operating points established, you should set down in writing, rules and regulations that will prevail for your league play. These would determine the method of selecting teams and the number of players on each team. Then you must determine if your league is to function in pubs, clubs, members' homes, or any combination of sites that would be available for league play. You must work up a regular schedule, both the length of your season and one or two nights of the week that the league is to meet for organized play sessions. Your rules should also include the official game or games to be played, the acceptable equipment for league play, a procedure for reporting results, and a method for filing protests.

Now that your league is in operation, each team should have a captain who is responsible for that team. The captains form the governing body of the league and at annual or more frequent meetings they discuss and take action on issues pertaining to running the league and changing any rules and regulations.

The league should have a recording secretary to handle recordkeeping and get information ready for whoever is responsible for preparing and distributing match-report sheets or newsletters that keep the members informed about the league.

Keep in mind that organized league play is an extremely enjoyable activity. It is one more way to increase your enjoyment of one of the most engrossing and relaxing sports known to man.

List of Organized Dart Leagues in the United States

Following is a list of major dart leagues and associations. For information about darting activity and leagues in areas not listed, write to the United States Darting Association, 516 Fifth Avenue, New York, NY 10036

Mens Dart Association
 of Anchorage
4332 Spenard Road
Anchorage, Alaska 99503

Womens Dart Association
 of Anchorage
4332 Spenard Road
Anchorage, Alaska 99503

Barbary Coast Professional Darts
 Association
5422 College Avenue
Oakland, California 94618

California Darts Federation
3721 Midvale Avenue
Los Angeles, California 90034

Central California Darts
Association
Post Office Box 1308
Monterey, California 93940

Channel Islands Dart League
946 Calle Cartito
Santa Barbara, California 93109

Pacific Darts Association
3208 West Ball Road
Anaheim, California 92804

Northern California Dart
Association
Post Office Box 4816
Hayward, California 94540

Sacramento Valley Darts
Association
8975 Woodward Way
Orange Valley, California 95662

Greater San Diego Darting
Association
Post Office Box 82131
San Diego, California 92138

San Francisco Dart League
269 Second Avenue
San Francisco, California 94118

Southern California Darts
Association
11119 West Washington
Boulevard
Culver City, California 90230

Tri-Counties Dart Conference
1530 North Coast Highway A
Laguna Beach, California 92651

Ventura Darts Association
Post Office Box 132
Port Hueneme, California 93041

Wednesday Night Dart Group
5422 College Avenue
Oakland, California 94618

Rocky Mountain Dart Association
4700 Cherry Creek Drive South
Denver, Colorado 80222

Connecticut Darting Association
Post Office Box 371
Old Saybrook, Connecticut 06475

U.S. Professional Dart
Association
1343 Connecticut Avenue N.W.
Washington, D.C. 20036

Washington Area Darts
Association
200 P Street N.W., Suite 500,
Washington, D.C. 20036

Dart Association of Palatka
Post Office Box 516
San Mateo, Florida 32088

Atlanta Darts Association
Post Office Box 52688
Atlanta, Georgia 30305

Hawaii Darts Association
2131 Kalakaua PH2
Honolulu, Hawaii 96815

Chicago Area Associated Darters
121 Custer Street
Evanston, Illinois 60207

Midwest Darters Club
6325 North Sheridan Road 1203
Chicago, Illinois 60626

Three Rivers Darting Association
5252-11 Stonehedge Boulevard
Fort Wayne, Indiana 46815

Cabbage Patch Darting Club
Greenville Junction
Greenville Junction, Maine 04442

Loring Dart Team
4101 Central Wyoming Avenue
Loring AFB, Maine 04751

Baltimore Area Darting
   Association
Post Office Box 5554
Towson, Maryland 21204

Minute Man Dart League
163 Harvard Avenue
Alston, Massachusetts 02134

Western Massachusetts Dart
   League
Walker Street
Lenoxdale, Massachusetts 01242

Ann Arbor Darts Association
600 West Washington
Ann Arbor, Michigan 48103

Detroit Open Dart League
1005 East Eleven Mile
Royal Oak, Michigan 48067

Greater Detroit Dart League
8385 Kennedy Circle
Warren, Michigan 48093

Wolverine Dart Association
Post Office Box 39051
Detroit, Michigan 48239

Twin City Darts Association
Post Office Box 23184
Richfield, Minnesota 55423

Missouri Darting Association
6529 Bonita
St. Louis, Missouri 63105

St. Louis Area Darts Association
7727 Keswick
St. Louis, Missouri 63119

Central Jersey English Dart
   League
430 Edgar Road
Elizabeth, New Jersey 07202

Garden State Dart Association
819 Lalor Street
Trenton, New Jersey 08610

Raritan Bay Dart League
28 West 11th Street
Linden, New Jersey 07036

Tippler's Dart Association
2932 Hyder S.E.
Albuquerque, New Mexico 87106

Greater Queens Dart League
74-17 46th Avenue
Elmhurst, New York 11373

Jelly Belly Dart Association
131 Third Street
Greenport, New York 11944

Long Island Darting Association
15 Jeffrey Lane
Hicksville, New York 11801

Metro Dart League
46 Gold Street
New York, New York 10038

Knickerbocker Darts
30 East 20th Street
New York, New York 10003

Southern Tier Dart Association
506 Church Street
Endicott, New York 13760

Suffolk County Dart League
90 West Main Street
Babylon, New York 11702

Triangle Dart League
300 Atlantic Avenue
Greenport, New York 11944

Queen City Darting Association
Post Office Box 15053
Charlotte, North Carolina 28210

Triangle Darting Association
909 Greenwood Road
Chapel Hill, North Carolina 27541

Central Ohio Darters
941 Chatham Lane
Columbus, Ohio 43219

Cleveland Darter Club
Post Office Box 81062
Cleveland, Ohio 44118

Dayton Darting Association
5641 King Arthur Drive
Centerville, Ohio 45429

Goosetown Astonishers Dart
Club
5 East Second Street
Chillicothe, Ohio 45601

Shamrock Darters Club
Grant Avenue at Naghten Street
Columbus, Ohio 43215

Southern Ohio Darting
Association
10931 Corona Road
Cincinnati, Ohio 45240

Mid-Willamette Valley Dart
League
1059 West 16th Street
Albany, Oregon 97321

Oregon Dart Association
12611 Southeast McLoughlin
Boulevard
Portland, Oregon 97222

Salem Dart Association
4684 Buckhorn Court
Salem, Oregon 97301

Bucks/Mont Dart League
1247 Ridge Road
Sellersville, Pennsylvania 18960

Delco Dart Association
104 Mildred Avenue
Collingsdale, Pennsylvania 19023

Greater Delaware Valley Darting
Association
961 Marcella Street
Philadelphia, Pennsylvania 19124

N.E. Community Dart League
6001 Edmund Street
Philadelphia, Pennsylvania 10134

Philadelphia English Dart League
327 South 13th Street
Philadelphia, Pennsylvania 19007

Pittsburgh Dart Association
4319 Penn Avenue
Pittsburgh, Pennsylvania 15224

Quaker City English Dart League
1413 East Cheltenham Ave.
Philadelphia, Pa. 19124

Women of Philadelphia English
  Darting League
3743 Frankford Avenue
Philadelphia, Pa. 19134

Greenville Dart Association
2084 Crosscrock Lane
Greenville, South Carolina 92607

Dallas Dart Association
Post Office Box 19404
Dallas, Texas 75219

Houston Dart Association
Post Office Box 452
Houston, Texas 77001

Metro Plex Darting Association
Post Office Box 4105
Irving, Texas 75061

San Antonio Dart League
6961 SPT. SQ.
Box 18874
San Antonio, Texas 78243

Texarkana Darts Association
Post Office Box 1852
Texarkana, Texas 75501

Salt Lake City Dart League
Box 2277
Salt Lake City, Utah 84110

Border Zone Dart League
Box 545
Newport, Vermont 05855

Hampton Area Dart Association
2084 Cunningham Drive #201
Hampton, Virginia 23666

Tidewater Area Dart Association
810 Lemaster Avenue
Hampton, Virginia 23669

Seattle Darts Association
16751 North Park Avenue
Seattle, Washington 98133

INDEX